Becoming Your DREAM

Bonnie Etta, PhD

YOUR DREAMED FUTURE IS POSSIBLE

Becoming Your Dream

This book is written to provide information and motivation to readers. Its purpose is not to render any type of psychological, legal, or professional advice of any kind. The content is the sole opinion and expression of the author, and not necessarily that of the publisher.

Copyright © 2023 by Bonnie Etta, PhD.

All rights reserved. No part of this book may be reproduced, transmitted, or distributed in any form by any means, including, but not limited to, recording, photocopying, or taking screenshots of parts of the book, without prior written permission from the author or the publisher. Brief quotations for noncommercial purposes, such as book reviews, permitted by Fair Use of the U.S. Copyright Law, are allowed without written permissions, as long as such quotations do not cause damage to the book's commercial value. For permissions, write to the publisher, whose address is stated below.

Printed in the United States of America.

ISBN   978-1-64552-174-7   (Paperback)
ISBN   978-1-64552-173-0   (Digital)

Lettra Press books may be ordered through booksellers or by contacting:

Lettra Press LLC
30 N Gould St. Suite 4753
Sheridan, WY 82801
1 307-200-3414 | info@lettrapress.com
www.lettrapress.com

TABLE OF CONTENTS

Preface v
Dedication ix

Chapter 1 God's Dream for You 1
Chapter 2 The Father's Heart 35
Chapter 3 The Passion of the Son 57
Chapter 4 Fulfilling Your Dream 70
Chapter 5 Recreating Your Future 82
Chapter 6 Breaking The Cage 110
Chapter 7 The Moses and the Joshua generation 122
Chapter 8 Walking In Divine Authority 138
Chapter 9 Prospering in crisis times 150

Notes 157
About the Author 161
About the book 163

PREFACE

Know what you want in life and go for it with all your spirit. Be determined to avoid the distractions in life. Be prepared to fight through the storms of life. Make up your mind to realize your dream no matter what it takes.

Hard work without appropriate knowledge only results to unprofitable labor and wasted years. Un-invested intelligence is as an un-mined field. Wise investment and commitment are intelligent steps towards recreating your future and becoming your dream. **It will take a healthy head and a healthy heart to produce a healthy and fruitful life; and only a healthy life can cautiously plan, pursue and walk towards a well defined future.**

Nelson Mandela is our twenty first century example; he stood the test of time and defied all oppositions, obstacles and suffering; nothing could kill or replace his dream.

In my twenty three years of teaching and counseling, and extensive traveling across the continents; I have come to understand that success is not determined by one's nationality or family name. Nobody can inherit success, you have to work it out as well as learn how to develop and maintain it.

You can become your dream: this book is a divine provision to assist you with divine intelligence and to develop in you the right attitude and courage towards realizing the dreams of your heart.

Don't give up; you can become your dream.

One day I decided to quit, I quit my job, my relationship, my spirituality. I wanted to quit my life.

I went to the woods to have one last talk with God. "God", I asked, "Can you give me one good reason why I should not quit? His answer surprised me... "Look around", He said. "Do you see the fern and the bamboo?" "Yes", I replied. "When I planted the fern and the bamboo seeds, I took very good care of them. I gave them light. I gave them water.

The fern quickly grew from the earth. Its brilliant green covered the floor. Yet nothing came from the bamboo seed. But I did not quit on the bamboo. In the second year the Fern grew more vibrant and plentiful. And again, nothing came from the bamboo seed. But I did not quit on the bamboo. He said. "In year three there was still nothing from the bamboo seed. But I would not quit. In year four, again, there was nothing from the bamboo seed. I would not quit." He said.

"Then in the fifth year a tiny sprout emerged from the earth. Compared to the fern it was seemingly small and insignificant... But just 6 months later the bamboo rose to over 100 feet tall. It had spent the five years growing roots. Those roots made it strong and gave it what it needed to survive. I would not give any of my creations a challenge it could not handle."

He asked me. "Did you know, my child, that all this time you have been struggling, you have actually been growing roots". "I would not quit on the bamboo. I will never quit on you." "Don't compare yourself to others." He said. "The bamboo had a different purpose than the fern. Yet they both make the forest beautiful." "Your time will come", God said to me. "You will rise high" "How high should I rise?" I asked. "How high will the bamboo rise?" He asked in return. "As high as it can?" I questioned. "Yes." He said, "Give me glory by rising as high as you can." I left the forest and brought back this story…

I hope these words can help you see that God will never give up on you. Never give up on your dream. Don't tell the Lord how big the problem is; tell the problem how Great your God is!

DEDICATION

I dedicate this book to all my partners and friends in ministry, that has greatly contributed to making my dream come true.

Waoh! This is a book to read and to share with friends.

I feel so privileged to have been given the opportunity to read this book. I have really been inspired and motivated to embark on three specific projects that I believe the Lord has always impressed upon my heart. We are blessed to be a blessing and I am happy to be a partner with this great vision.

Dr Patricia N. Ayuk.

CHAPTER ONE

God's Dream for You

"To appoint unto them that mourn in Zion, to give unto them beauty for ashes, the oil of joy for mourning, the garment of praise for the spirit of heaviness; that they might be called trees of righteousness, the planting of the LORD, that he might be glorified"*

GOD'S DREAM FOR YOU

I am a father of four sons, I call them world changers, and these children are precious to me. My heart yearns for the joy, success and wellbeing of my Children. Isn't it wonderful to consider our heavenly father's dream for us his children? It's time to take hold of the Father's vision for your life. I want us to examine His heart beat for you personally.

The scriptures clearly reveal to us the Father's heart, and deepest desire for His children:

> "For thou art an holy people unto the LORD thy God: the LORD thy God hath chosen thee to be a special people unto himself, above all people that are upon the face of the earth".*

You are special before the Lord; you are distinguished from all other creation around you. For the Lord has chosen you to be holy, separated unto Him. You should know the place and value God placed on you, you are God's ultimate heart's desire, and without you the love of God has no meaning. Without you the whole creation has no value, for you are God's master-piece on earth.

You are created by design, as He is so are you in Christ Jesus, created in His own image and likeness. You are so special, chosen, unique and distinguished; Separated unto the will of the Lord for His divine pleasure. You are not a product of evolution. Your life has a special purpose and that is fulfilling God's desire; being one with God for his purpose for humanity and eternity.

"The LORD hath appeared of old unto me, *saying,* Yea, I have loved thee with an everlasting love: therefore with loving-kindness have I drawn thee".*

Can you hear the Lord singing a love song to you? He is saying, 'I Love you with everlasting love, He is saying to you, my son, my precious daughter, my love for you has no limit. You are the reason for all creation.

The Father wants you to personally experience His infinite love.

You are loved. His love is not based upon your good deeds and accomplishments. His love is based upon who you are. You are precious and priceless. You are the reason for all creation; you are the heart beat of God.

God wants you to receive his love, accept his love for you, personally. His gift for you is His love. His love comes along with his mercy and compassion. His grace brought to us the gift of His Son; His Son brought to us the gift of eternal life, eternal life brought to us all that pertain to life and godliness. Eternal life brought to us the gift of the abundant life through His word.

This is the greatest manifestation of love. You are loved; you are the beloved of the Lord. Your love is the greatest worship He requires from you. Walk in His love, dwell in His love and shine forth His love to the world around you. Love that is concealed is dead, love can not be hidden. Love is like yeast, "a little leaven, leaveneth the whole lump".* Affect your world with His love. Be possessed with the spirit of the love of God. Think love, dream love, speak love and display the love of God. Love is care.

God revealed and demonstrated his love through Christ Jesus. God demonstrates his love for us everyday of our lives, for His mercies are new everyday. Great is His faithfulness.

How do you manifest love?

How do you demonstrate the love of God which you have received, to your friends, family and community? Find ways to express the love of Christ daily; make it a duty just to show someone that Jesus loves them through you. Your world is yearning for the love of Christ through you. Share love to the staving world.

The greatest cure to our world's problems is genuine love. People are sick of the lack of love. There is hate everywhere, the news media all day long feed the public with disasters and conflicts, and little good news is presented through the mainstream media stations. In Christ there is real love.

Love is taking care of the poor and needy.
Love is reaching out to widows and orphans.
Love is sharing your faith with someone.
Love is caring for the abused and rejected.
Love is feeding the hungry.
Love is assisting an abandoned child with school fees.
Love is being in partnership with ministries for the salvation of souls.
Love is healing hearts, wiping tears and giving hope.
Love is giving a smile to someone in pain.
His dream is to see you love as He has loved you.
Just love, let's love.
Through love, give someone the reason to celebrate life.
Through love, lift up a broken and bruised soul.

Through love, embrace a lonely and disappointed child.
Through love, share your joy with the oppressed and the poor.

God wants you to experience his power and glory.

"The eyes of your understanding being enlightened; that ye may know what is the hope of his calling and what the riches of the glory of his inheritance in the saints. And what *is* the exceeding greatness of his power to us-ward who believe, according to the working of his mighty power".*

Our God is the Almighty God, yet many live as if the Lord God is not able to perform. It is sad to say that many children of God have not seen the power and the glory of the God they believe in. You are not just called to believe in the power of God but to demonstrate that power daily as you deal with challenging situations of life, Child of God; it is His heart's desire for you to carry his power and to see Him manifest His power and glory in and through you to positively affect change in your community.

His dream is to see you empowered by his infinite supernatural miracle working power. You were not born to live helpless, hopeless and powerless.

God is glorified in you when you walk and live endued with the heavenly power for the advancement of the kingdom of God on earth.

Powerless Christianity is dead religion.

A powerless Christian is a victim and a noise maker, the works of the wicked will continually advance in our world because of empty religious Christianity that has no power to break down the kingdom of darkness. God wants to empower you to do exploits and better represent Him in your community and in His kingdom.

The power of God is available for you. The Father wants you to personally experience and carry his indwelling and manifest power. The Lord has the power to save, He is mighty to save. The same power that raised Jesus Christ from the dead is able to save you to the uttermost.

> "Wherefore he is able also to save them to the uttermost that come unto God by him, seeing He ever liveth to make intercession for them".*

I speak into your present situation right now.
The Lord will save you, you will not sink but you will rise up powerfully in the name of the Lord Jesus Christ.
The Lord will save your family and He will give you a life of testimonies.

He is able to save you from the tribulations around you: just believe and call upon Him with simple faith. Never lose heart, there is still hope. His saving grace will change the story of your life. He has the power to intervene in issues concerning your marriage, your finances, your job and your career. He is the Lord our Savior, He will come and save you. Call onto Him with simple faith.

Today begin to meditate on the power and glory of God.
Fill your mind with the divine ability of your God.
Confess and declare publicly the power of your God upon your life. Anticipate the manifestation of the power and glory of God in every situation you come across today.

See the Lord Jesus Christ, as a very present help in times of need. He is ever present, capable and available to save. Feed yourself with faith scriptures that deal with the power and glory of God.

Noah in the Bible experienced God's power in the flood. He saw the love and mercy of God for his family and for his life.

He saw the power of God that sustained him and his family in a time of global crisis. It is important for you to know and believe that God will sustain you in times of national and global crisis; your story will be different in times of hardship and crisis. Your God will preserve and bless you and make you a living testimony.

Noah saw the power of God in the obedience of the animals. The wild animals answered the call of God for their salvation. And they came in, male and female for the continuity of their posterity.

Noah saw the power of God in that his wife and children were not disobedient to the word of the Lord, all of them responded to the call and were a part of the construction of the ark for their safety. None of Noah's children disbelieved the word of the Lord from the mouth of their father.

The Lord will grant you the grace to raise up a blessed and redeemed family. A family of faith and trust in the name of the Lord.

You will see the power of God in your life in the name of Jesus.

You will see the power of God in your area of ministry in the mighty name of Jesus. The same power that protected Noah and all the animals in the ark will protect and keep you; God will protect and keep alive everything that will make your life, your career and ministry complete and effective in the name of Jesus Christ, until you see the fulfillment of that dream of your heart.

Confess these aloud and with all boldness:

The power of God will work on my behalf.
The power of God will open doors for me.
The power of God will subdue all the enemies before me.
The power of God will break every stronghold and remove every obstacle before me.
The power of God will cause me to dance and testify of the goodness of my God.
The power of God will take me to my desired end, and cause my dreams to come to pass.
The power of God will protect and hide me from all the snares of the wicked.
The power of God will keep me alive and well in the name of Jesus Christ.

It will take the manifest power of God for you to live happy and safe in the midst of this wicked and perverse generation.

It will take the power and grace of God for you to raise your children in the fear of the Lord and to keep them save from the corruption in the neighborhood.

It will take the power of God for you to grow the ministry that is placed in your care, and it will take the power of God for your ministry to get breakthrough in your community.

It will take the power of God for you to break the powers of principalities and powers in the air, and for your business explosion. You will need the power of God to win the battles of life.

> "For we wrestle not against flesh and blood but against principalities and against rulers and against spiritual wickedness in heavenly places".*

Right now, I declare total defeat of every spiritual authority that is standing on your way to success in the name of Jesus Christ. I declare the down fall of every demonic agent that is assigned to hinder your vision and investment in the name Jesus Christ.

I declare your total victory, and your total freedom. I declare your season of testimonies in the name of Jesus.

Confess these verses aloud:

> "No weapon that is formed against me shall prosper; and every tongue that shall rise against me in judgment i shalt condemn. This is the heritage of the servants of the LORD, and their righteousness is of me, saith the LORD".*

> "And he said unto them, I beheld Satan as lightning fall from heaven. Behold, I give unto you power to tread on serpents and scorpions, and over all the power of the enemy: and nothing shall by any means hurt you".*

Right now, let the power of Jesus Christ begin to move all over your body for total healing and restoration.

I rebuke every pain and every disease in your body in the name of Jesus Christ.

I command every infirmity to die in your body and command you to rise up and be healed right now in the name of Jesus.

I speak a release of the power of God in your job and I speak a total turn around for good in every area of your life. Things must change for good in the name of Jesus.

I speak a release of the power of God in your family; let the power of the Holy Spirit begin to work for the healing and restoration of your marriage and for the transformation of your children, in the name of Jesus Christ.

I pray for a fresh release of the power of God in your ministry, let the Power of the Holy Spirit make a difference in every area of commitment that concerns you in the name of Jesus Christ. Connect to the power of God for your testimony right now in the name of Jesus Christ.

I was in Babong Village, somewhere in central Africa with my brother Etta Philip, and by eleven pm there was a cry of hopelessness and desperation. A young lady was in bitter cry, her two days old baby was dying of tetanus, and the nearest clinic to Babong village was four to five hours on foot. The whole family was in confusion and in total despair. The little child was stretching to die and all hopes were lost.

Because of the cry I and my brother left our room in haste and literally ran to the neighborhood to see what was going on. Seeing the baby, my heart was filled with pain and I took the child in my arms, together with my brother, we just said Jesus, Jesus, and Jesus, do it again. Suddenly the child fell asleep and the parents thought the child was dead. We handed the child over to the mom with instructions to let her sleep, the child got up from sleep early the next morning totally fine and strong. Alleluia.

The power of God touched the child and brought total healing from the deadly disease. This is your day. Receive your testimony now in the name of Jesus Christ. Your faith in Jesus Christ will surely produce great results. See Jesus doing it for you, Jesus is real and is willing to be glorified in your situation today.

The Father wants you to experience His tangible presence.

I asked the Lord, "why do so many people attend church but never get to any tangible change in their lives"?

"Why do so many pastors and missionaries die in mission fields afflicted and defeated"?

"Lord, why do so many 'Christians' suffer because of spiritual wickedness and demonic attacks"?

And the Lord made me to understand that the people suffer defeats because of *'the absence of His presence'*.

There are many activities going on today in the name of the Lord, but without the Lord having anything to do with them.

There are so many professing Christians today, but without the indwelling Christ in them.

There are so many theological pastors and Bishops, but without the experience of Pentecost.

Many are working for God but without God. They use their might and intellect. They depend on their experiences, secular education and traditions of their church fathers. They depend on science and technology, but have no relationship with the Spirit of the living God. All our efforts without the active presence of the Spirit and presence of God, cannot achieve our spiritual goals. We need the presence of the Spirit of God in every day life.

The Father wants you to experience and live by His presence.

His presence will cause you to move forward in life without fears.

His presence will cause you to progress in the midst of opposition and satanic resistance.

His presence will make you fruitful, like a tree planted by rivers of water.

The presence of the Lord in your home will give you blessed family and peace.

His presence is sweet and precious sleep, with nothing to oppress your spirit.

His presence is blessedness and favor; you shall be like the palm tree.

His presence is joy and peace; He will give you a song in the night.

His presence is victory and testimonies; I declare your season of testimony has come in Jesus name.

His presence is diverse opportunities.

His presence is wisdom for life.

His presence is health, wellbeing and soundness.

His presence is love and abundant life.

His presence is deep assurance and divine insurance.

His presence is salvation.

Do you have His presence with you? For without His presence, you will die before your time.

The devil is not afraid of your tittles and degrees, he is not afraid of your professional skills, he is not afraid of your bible knowledge; he is not afraid of your church affiliation nor is he afraid of your relationship to the senior pastor.

You cannot stop the evil one with your communion card, nor with your membership card. Your baptism card cannot drive away the presence of the evil one.

You cannot stop the devil with your involvement in church activities; you can not stop the evil one with a form of godliness without the power of God. You need to be overshadowed by the presence of God. You need to carry His presence and Anointing. You have suffered for so long because of His absence, surrender to Him and allow Him to be the Lord of your life. "For as many as are led by the Spirit, they are the sons of God".*

Don't leave your room without His presence going along with you.
Don't leave your house without His presence going with you.
Don't make decisions and engagements without His presence working through you and in you.
Don't climb the pulpit without His presence upon you. "The letter killeth but the Spirit giveth life".*

Five dimensions of God's presence.
THE OMNIPRESENCE OF GOD

He is every where as a witness, nothing is hidden from Him. But God's omnipresence is inactive to our personal experience. He is in heaven and in hell. He is in churches and in casinos. God's omnipresence cannot stop a thief from stealing. It cannot stop the wicked from his wicked intensions. We are not be saved by God's omnipresence.

God's Omnipresence is not experienced individually; one cannot get a personal experience of His Omnipresence. One cannot get encounter with God's Omnipresence. You need much more than the Omnipresence of God. As the fish in the Ocean cannot get a special encounter with water, since it dwells in the midst of it. So we dwell in the presence of God. He is all around us and no one can run away from God's presence. No man can hide from God; He is there and always there, Jehovah Shamah. Child of God, you are never alone; His presence is always there where ever you are, God is there for you.

> "Thus saith the LORD, the heaven is my throne, and the earth is my footstool: where is the house that ye build unto me? And where is the place of my rest"?*

THE ABIDING PRESENCE OF GOD

Immanuel, God with us. The abiding presence of God is: External abiding presence for divine interventions, divine strengthening, divine information and divine guidance, etc. This can be for the saved and even the unsaved. God's presence can be with a run-away son because of the mother's intercession for protection, salvation and for divine intervention. God's presence is what brings conviction of sins for salvation and regeneration. God's presence has been with our soldiers on the battle fronts and rescued them from death because of the prayers of the church. Listen to their stories and you would hear how God intervened for them and saved them miraculously. Every soldier who has been engaged in war and returned safe and sound believes in miracles.

> *'Even* the Spirit of truth; whom the world cannot receive, because it seeth him not, neither knoweth him: but ye know him; for he dwelleth with you, and shall be in you'.*

He dwells *with* you and shall be *in* you.
You need much more than His abiding presence.

HE INDWELLING PRESENCE OF GOD

The Indwelling presence of God is only for the redeemed of the Lord, for those who are washed and sanctified by the Blood of the Lamb.
This is the purpose of the Baptism of the Holy Spirit. The Holy Spirit now comes and makes His abode in us and we then become the temples of the living God. The Holy Spirit does not dwell in unclean vessels.

"Jesus answered and said unto him, if a man loves me, he will keep my words: and my Father will love him, and we will come unto him, and make our abode with him.
He that loveth me not keepeth not my sayings: and the word which ye hear is not mine, but the Father's which sent me".*
"And we are his witnesses of these things; and so is also the Holy Ghost, whom God hath given to them that obey him".*

One of the greatest privileges I have in life is the indwelling presence of God in me. All I have is His presence; His presence is life, His presence is glory and the Anointing for life. His presence is the secret of the success of my life and ministry.
You cannot afford to live void of His presence anymore. It's not too late; even now it can happen, you can be filled to overflowing; right now drop the book and go on your knees and ask Him to baptize you with the Holy Spirit. Empty yourself and let Him in, let Him fill you completely with his power and glory. There is emptiness and un-fulfillment in you that only He can satisfy; let Him in today and your life will have new meaning and overflowing experience of joy unspeakable.
His presence is not a product of water baptism. His presence is not gotten through religious confirmations and ordinations.

There are so many ordained ministers who are carnal and empty. They cause more problems in the kingdom than the solutions and answers they were called to provide. You need the indwelling presence of the Holy Spirit in you.

THE MANIFEST PRESENCE OF GOD

The world cannot see the Omnipresence of God; they cannot see the abiding presence of God. People in your family and community cannot see the indwelling presence of God. But when people see the manifest power of God, they know God is God and that God is with you.

Remember Elijah and the prophets of Baal, when the people saw the fire coming down from heaven and consume the sacrifice of Elijah, then they all shouted and praised the God of Israel and their faith in Him was revived.

It was the manifest presence of God that was displayed in Egypt that brought king pharaoh to his knees; all his gods failed him. He saw the power and the glory of the God of Israel. King Pharaoh saw the manifestation of the God of Israel and knew the difference between the real and the false gods and he requested for prayers of blessings from Moses.

It was the manifest presence of God that caused the children of Israel to cross over the Red sea on dry ground. They witnessed the manifest power of God and the destruction of the gods and armies of king Pharaoh and they knew that the God of Israel fought for his people.

The Lord our God will manifest his power for your deliverance in the name of Jesus Christ.

The Lord will manifest for your breakthrough in the name of the Lord Jesus Christ.

The Lord your God will manifest for your open doors in the name of Jesus Christ.

The Lord God will manifest His glory and power for your children and for your posterity.

Today, I confess in the name of Jesus Christ; the Son of God that the Lord will manifest for your prosperity and for your financial breakthrough for the sake of the advancement of the kingdom of God.

You will see the power of God for total change in your condition and situation in the name of Jesus Christ.

It was the manifest presence of God that brought Jericho to total defeat and destruction. The God of Israel showed up for his people and pushed down the great walls of Jericho.

Every wall that the enemy has raised up on your way, to hinder and to limit, today let that wall collapse in the name of Jesus Christ. Let every obstacle give way for your advancement, let the mountains before you become plains and let there be a way for you even through the wilderness.

Have you ever seen the actions of the God you have believed? A God that does not act is an idol. Our God is alive and well and active. The blind see, the deaf hear the lame walk, the dead are raised and lives are being transformed daily in the name of Jesus Christ of Nazareth.

If your God depends on you to take care of him then change your God. Our God takes care of us. We don't labor to sustain our God; our God sustains the entire world by His infinite Word. He will take care of all that concerns you, fear no more, cling to Him and see His glory and power.

The season has come for the Lord to manifest for your uncommon testimony, believe it and call on the name of Jesus Christ for help. Make Jesus Christ your source and He will never fail you.

God wants you to experience the overshadowing of His presence.

"And the angel answered and said unto her, The Holy Ghost shall come upon thee and the power of the Highest shall overshadow thee: therefore also that holy thing which shall be born of thee shall be called the Son of God"*.

"While he thus spake, there came a cloud, and overshadowed them: and they feared as they entered into the cloud".* "And Moses went into the midst of the cloud, and gat him up into the mount: and Moses was in the mount forty days and forty nights".*

God wants to envelope you with his presence: He wants you to dwell in 'God as God is in you'. You in him and He in you forever. What a wonderful fellowship and intimacy.

God is calling you for a baptism, you being entirely immersed in his glory and presence. From today, let His presence overshadow your whole being in the name of Jesus Christ.

Today; just dive into the ocean of God's presence and swim deep.

God wants you to experience His faithfulness.

I have been privileged to listen to the angels sing several times. The last time I was part of the Angelic choir it was an inexplicable experience, how I longed to remain in that atmosphere of peace, tranquility and life. This is what the Angels were singing:

"Jesus: the Faithful God.
Jesus: The Almighty God.

Jesus: The Able God.
Jesus: The Truthful God.
Jesus: The Reliable God.
Jesus: The Unchangeable God.
Jesus: The Holy one.
Jesus: The Prince of peace.
Jesus: The Most High God.
Jesus: The All wise God.
Jesus: The Lord of lords.
Jesus: The King of kings.
Amen-Amen- Amen".

God wants you to experience His faithfulness. You can never fully understand how faithful He is, until you are fully overshadowed by His presence. Only by the Holy Spirit can we intimately know and understand the dept of God's faithfulness to us all. My dear friend, rely on His faithfulness; know that all can fail but not God. Just surrender to Him and let Him drive your life through His word. With Him you will surely reach your destination without chaos.

Tell yourself; 'my God is the faithful God. I will see God's faithfulness in every area of my life. My God will never fail me'.

"I will extol thee, O LORD; for thou hast lifted me up, and hast not made my foes to rejoice over me. O LORD my God, I cried unto thee and thou hast healed me. O LORD, thou hast brought up my soul from the grave: thou hast kept me Alive; that I should not go down to the pit. Sing unto the LORD, O ye saints of his, and give thanks at the remembrance of his holiness. For his anger *endureth but* a moment; in his favour *is* life: weeping may endure for a night, but joy *cometh* in the morning. And in my prosperity I said, I shall never be moved. LORD, by thy favour thou hast made my mountain to stand strong: thou didst hide thy face, *and* I was troubled. I cried to thee, O LORD; and unto the LORD I made supplication. What profit *is there* in my blood, when I go down to the pit?

Shall the dust praise thee? Shall it declare thy truth? Hear,
O LORD, and have mercy upon me: LORD, be thou my helper.
    Thou hast turned for me my mourning into dancing:
Thou hast put off my sackcloth, and girded me with gladness;
    To the end that *my* glory may sing praise to thee, and not be silent.
O LORD my God, I will give thanks unto thee forever".*

GOD WANTS YOU TO EXPERIENCE HIS BLESSINGS.

"The LORD hath been mindful of us: He will bless *us*; he will
    bless the house of Israel; he will bless the house of Aaron.
He will bless them that fear the LORD, *both* small and great.
The LORD shall increase you more and more, you and Your
    children.
Ye *are* blessed of the LORD which made heaven and earth.
The heaven, even the heavens, are the LORD'S: but the earth
    hath he given to the children of men".*

    All that God has is for His children. The blessing is being a partaker of your heavenly Father's wealth. This has to manifest in every area of your life. It is the Father's desire that you be blessed beyond human comprehension.

    The blessing should affect you Spiritually, Socially, Mentally, Morally, intellectually and economically. Deficiency in any of these areas is the reason for pain, distress and confusion and unhappiness. You have the right through the blood of Jesus Christ for all that belongs to God your Father. You are not born again to be a curse and abuse in society; you are too blessed to be cursed.

If you live as though you are cursed, it is due to your spiritual ignorance of the finished work of Jesus Christ on the cross for you. You have a choice to walk in the blessings of the Lord Jesus Christ our redeemer or to depend on your own strength and ability. Your wages of twenty years of hard labor can never be compared to the blessing the Lord is able to pour upon your life in one year. Your prosperity is not based upon how much you earn but upon how much you save and invest.

Let every devourer of your finances be destroyed today in the name of Jesus Christ. Your money will be spent correctly and purposefully invested in well planed projects.

The Father wants to see you blessed and happy. He has made all the provision for your blessedness and for your wellbeing. When He gave His only begotten Son Jesus Christ to die as a sacrifice for all mankind; the Father through the death of his only Son has qualified all who put their faith in the blood of Jesus Christ His Son for the blessings and grace. This blessing through the precious blood of Jesus Christ is the key to our health and peace, security and abundant life. No one can curse you as long as you are washed by the blood of Jesus Christ.

The blood of Jesus is the only means by which man can have access to heaven for all the Father's treasures. The blood of Jesus is the key to the store house of God. Through the blood of Jesus Christ you are qualified for all of God's blessings, keep reminding yourself. Tell yourself I am qualified for the blessings of my heavenly Father. Keep talking to yourself; all that belongs to God belongs to me, for I am his precious child in Christ Jesus. I am the heir of God through Christ Jesus. I am the blessed of the Lord God. I am blessed for life.

I declare a new day of favor and grace for you and your family in the name of Jesus.

The blessings of God will change the story of your life from this day forward. Your job will be a blessing and the works of your hands will bring great reward and satisfaction.

You will be a light to your community and a voice to your nation. You are moving only forward and never backward in the name of the Lord Jesus Christ.

The blessing of the Lord will manifest in and through you. It will manifest for you and on you. The world around you will witness the tangible blessings of God in your life. It is time to walk in the fullness of the blessing; it is the heart beat of your heavenly Father to see you full of joy and excitement. The Father is well-pleased as you live and walk in the fullness of the blessings of the sacrifice of Jesus Christ on the cross of Calvary.

Be blessed and remain a blessing to your world.

In your blessing, don't forget the poor and the needy.

In your blessing, don't forget lost souls, invest in evangelistic projects, don't forget sponsoring missions and missionaries.

In your blessing, don't forget the widows and the fatherless.

GOD'S DREAM FOR YOU IS TO MAKE THE BEST OUT OF YOU.

You were not created for junk. Don't go for junk.

You were not created to mourn. Don't go for that which will bring failure and headaches.

You were not created to be used and abandoned. Never use your life for experiment.

You were created for God. Worship and serve God as the only reason for your living.

You were created with value and dignity. Never dishonor and devaluate yourself.

You were created by design, live for excellence.

You were created for the best; for you are the best of the creation. Nothing can be compared to you in the entire universe. All the things around you were created for you, all were created to serve you and to enable you to live life fully in order to serve God and give Him all the glory in return.

It is time to manifest, to bring forth the excellence in you. Don't go for anything; go for something, something reasonable before God and for the advancement of your life. There is nothing around you that is worthy of your life, don't die for a house, don't die for a job, don't die for money, don't die for fame, don't die for food, don't die for sex or for any human relationship and don't die for religion. Only God is worthy for you to live and to die for.

Let your life fulfill God's dream for your existence. Live to make heaven glad, live to heal hearts, give hope and save souls through the love of Jesus Christ. Like Apostle Paul, live for the salvation of souls, and be prepared to live and die for the glory of God.

MEDITATION.

How I overcame the battle with insomnia.

It all began when my parents separated and my father later remarried. Surprisingly enough, I was the most traumatized among all four siblings. One afternoon I had to take a nap in the guest room to avoid the noise from the room I shared with my other sisters. While in that guest room, my mind kept plunging into all sorts of bitter thoughts against my father for what he had done to my mother. I found myself feeding my mind with negative thoughts and resentment against my dad and my step mother. My mother had worked so hard to build up a family and to establish my dad's career, but now a strange woman had stepped in, pushed out my mom to possess everything.

I remember that it was about twelve in the afternoon, that I went into the room to rest; but from that hour until about 2.am my thoughts were only thoughts of resentment towards my father. I had slept for about forty-five minutes when all of a sudden sleep completely dried up from my eyes. And then from that moment and day in the year 1995, till about the end of 2004 I could not sleep.

It sounds incredible that someone would go on for such a long time without any sleep. But that was actually my experience. And when I talk about insomnia, I mean chronic insomnia in this case. I experienced absolute deficiency and inability to sleep. I mean zero degree sleep. In that year 1995, I was in an examination class preparing to write the Ordinary level exams (GCE O' levels). I was studying without any trace of sleep. Now what was unusual about this was that when I picked up my books to study, immediately I would feel sleepy but as soon as I rushed to bed sleep would vanish away. The situation deprived me from rest, I would lie on the bed for hours waiting and praying for just a little sleep but to no avail. That was when depression and worthlessness took over my life.

I began to feel lonely, resentful and aggressive towards every person who wasn't my direct sibling, but above all I was most resentful towards my dad and step mom. I harbored so much hatred in me for them in a way that one could feel it. After some months I began loosing weight and experienced unusual palpitation.

My heart was palpitating so hard that I was scared of sitting close to people; I felt they could hear my heart beats. Every time I held something, a teacup or glass of water trembled, my nerves were severely affected. With all what I was going through no one at home really understood the intensity of my suffering. I shared the same bed with one of my sisters, each morning I would get up and tell her that I could not sleep but because she could not understand how someone would go on and on without sleep she would always tell me I was lying.

It came to the point in my trauma that I became frightened every time the night was approaching. Because I knew I was going to keep watch while others enjoyed good night rest. Worse still I was sharing the same bed with my sister so I always was afraid the bed would be banging due to the severity of my heart beats. So every night I would sleep on my back in a tensed mood, with the effort to reduce the vibration.

Prior to all these I had informed my dad about my sleep situation. He being a medical doctor prescribed the best drugs which he knew could treat my illness. I remembered one of such drugs was the valium tablets. I was administered valium 5ms, which I took but it was ineffective. I went ahead to take the valium 10ms, but my body rejected the drug. Rather I got up each morning more depressed. It came to the point where everything about life lost meaning and secretly I began contemplating suicide.

I remember telling my dad that all the drugs he had administered to me were not working. He did administer more drugs but my situation did not change. Finally he told me he had no idea as to what he could do next for my case. I became embittered with him the more and every other person around me became a problem to me. I began plunging more and more into serious depression and despair. I resolved to over eating, and seeking for pleasures in wrong places to cover up the emptiness that was building inside of me. But it still did not work for good; because I was trying to fake happiness and joy which turned out to more frustration.

I consequently could not succeed in my exams that year and had to rewrite the next year. The pain of failure and the task of repeating the same class only served as fuel for my worsening heart condition. The insomnia had not been any better and still in that condition I had to study hard for my exams. That year by the grace of Jesus, I made it with five papers Ordinary Level, G.C.E. I was surprised and happy for my success and gave all the credits to my God. From that moment I decided to go on with life and the thoughts of suicide gradually began to give way.

However my sleeplessness worsened. I began reading books on how to overcome insomnia. I read a lot of magazines on health and the improvement of my diet. I read a lot of books written by psychologist on how to deal with insomnia. But let me remark here that they were all wonderful suggestions without any practical solution. I did all to practice what was suggested in these books but failed to achieve the results. For example they suggested aerobic exercises that were exceedingly tedious;

I tried them but still failed. I came across many psychologists' books which suggested that exercise was a wonderful therapy for insomniacs. In spite of little success with the exercises, I thank God for these books have helped me to acquire a desire for outdoor activities and exercise.

I went to high school in 1996 still in the same condition. In school I would talk with my school mates, laugh with them and walk home with them, but inside I was dying. Outside I manifested a kind of false gaiety and joy but pretending, because I did not want my friends to find out the dept of my frustration.

With every passing day my life got worse and my sleeplessness persisted. I was an empty mass moving around but I succeeded in concealing it so much that people did not know my real experience. The only remark they made was that I was losing weight and that I should do something about it. I became very frighten to move alone. I was scared of meeting people I have not seen for a while because it was obvious that they would mention my weight loss. However I put all my efforts to continue with my education.

Another phase of my sickness is that it pushed me into relapse. Life became so unbearable for me; I told my dad that if nothing was done about my situation I will drop down dead some day because I could no longer cope with the degree of stress. Another stage of depression set in, which manifested in a higher level of distraction and lack of concentration. I was so distracted in a way that I would read a paragraph of my notes over and over for a long time before I finally got to understanding what I was reading. I also did not care about what could happen to me, so I plunged into wrong relationships and did daring things that were very strange to my nature. I was consciously moving towards self destruction.

One day as I laid on my bed in my room wrestling with sleeplessness as usual, time elapse and I could not figure out where I was. I only realized myself prowling in the bathroom as if I was drunk. Then suddenly I knocked my chin on the railing on the wall of the bathroom where towels are hung and fell on the bathroom floor. I only realized myself early the next morning, before leaving to the hospital for a check up. I could not explain what actually happened.

That year I graduated from high school only by God's grace, but I did not register for the university because I wasn't ready to take on any kind of studies again except my situation got better. My mom was so worried about my situation that she said we should try a psychiatrist in the capital city. We visited the psychiatric center and I talked with the psychiatrist. I recounted to him my experiences. But all he did could not solve my problem.

I had developed fear of death and fear for the future. Every time I heard some one had died I got so scared because I thought I would be the next person to die. I was so scared of the future but could not understand why. All of these added to the trauma of unbearable palpitation. The psychiatrist listened to me and later on prescribed some drugs for me. Of course all that ended up with no positive results, nothing changed and I only got the more depressed.

By the year 1999 I personally began looking for all sorts of avenues to overcome insomnia. One night I found myself as in a dream, some one asked me this question; "so you really want peace?" And I said yes that was my heart's desire. And I remember the person talking to me in the dream, saying that the kind of peace I was looking for could never be found have through any other means, and that Jesus Christ was the only source of the kind of peace I desired. In other words he was saying that the only way for a solution to my problem was Jesus Christ. That night, I felt more frustrated than ever before.

Nobody around me understood my level of desperation, my sisters said I was lying all the time that I couldn't sleep, my father was tired of administering drugs and my mother also was at the point of breaking down. She thought of what to do and also trying to cope with the trauma of divorce. I didn't want to bother her any further, so I was left alone in my suffering. At this point I didn't have any relationship with Jesus Christ though I went to church occasionally, true faith in God was such a distant concept for me. Some friend began preaching and telling me how much I have been deceived by the devil.

I had followed religion and traditions but not Jesus. It was hard for me to understand that Christ Jesus had given us his peace and salvation when He died on the cross and now we could receive His peace, free if only we believed in Him as our personal Lord and Savior. This was totally unreasonable to me.

However at that moment in time, my painful experiences left me with more suicidal tendencies. Since no one believed in me anymore, I stopped explaining myself to people. The more I tried to explain my dilemma, they always concluded that it was unthinkable for anyone to go that long without any form of sleep.

One day, due to want of sleep and rest I decided I was going to seek counseling from the resident Pastor of the Church where I occasionally attended. I made an appointment to meet him in his office. In the course of that he gave me the usual suggestions and commandments to keep which I could not see how to go about practicing them. At the end of the counseling session he added to my already existing dilemma. I left his office more traumatized and condemned because of my sinful life, and I thought to myself, going to see that pastor in the first place was a mistake. I decided that it will never repeat itself again. In my heart I had already concluded there wasn't any hope in God.

During the academic year 1998, I changed my mind about loosing the whole year and not going to school. So I went in for a late entry and enrolled into the university, my health situation not withstanding. Prior to that I made up my mind I was going to do psychology so that with the knowledge I could gain from that, I could better analyze my health situation and seek out workable solutions for myself.

Studying without sleep was a nightmare and I went through higher education as if in a slow motion. I was experiencing fatigue 24 hours a day and chronic headaches that left me dizzy almost all the time. In school I began seeking for comfort by entering into unnecessary relationships and going to wild parties late in the night because I was trying to make up for the vacuum within me. I hated myself for doing all of what I was involved in, but I was enslaved to them because I needed to fill the worthlessness I felt about my life.

Yet again, while in school I relapsed into another phase of my fight with insomnia. Every time I went to bed I noticed that I began experiencing a bit of sleep and just when I began drowsing I would get a violent shake, as if some one actually used their hands to wake me up, and that would be the end of sleep for the rest of that night. I remember very vividly, I was in my room in the university hostel, it was about 6 pm and I had just come back from the class tired and feeling sick from lack of sleep. Immediately I fell on the bed and started struggling to fall asleep; at about 9 pm, I remember as I began experiencing sleep, suddenly I saw the picture of a huge lion coming towards me and then I woke up in fright and that was the end of sleep for that day.

At other times when I started to doze off I felt as if some one shook me violently and I fell off my bed to the floor. After all these experiences, I knew it was no longer just insomnia but some sort of demonic influence. To confirm this I went home during the first semester break, after spending time with the rest of our family members in the living room, I decided to have an early night.

Basically I knew that sleep for me was a forgone conclusion, so my going to bed that evening was basically to meditate. Minutes later I was caught up between sleep and wakefulness and instantly I found myself in a different environment in a dilapidated building but still on my bed. I was frightened and tried to scream but I could not. The only prayer I knew how to say by then was the Lord's Prayer "our father…". I began to recite the prayer inside of me; since I couldn't shout. The moment I began to pray, I immediately found myself back into my room and that was all for the night as far as sleep was concerned.

Now what began as insomnia at the initial stage had given birth to other forms of malaise for me. I was not just plagued by insomnia but great depression, phobia and other forms of spiritual occurrences such as some one shaking me violently when I was just about getting some sleep. And the picture of the wild lion moving towards me that would frighten me out of the slightest bit of sleep, etc.

Looking back now I do think that only the mercy and grace of God kept me through the horror of sleeplessness for all those years especially in such circumstances where I had to go through studies as well.

It was normal that anyone suffering from such adverse situation like I, ought to have been hospitalized or put under a lengthy period of psychotherapy. My personality was completely shattered, I had lost self esteem and I was full of fear. I kept asking myself "who am I, where do I go from here, what next…"

From the period I enrolled into the university 1998 to 2002, I experienced the same frustration with increasing intensity as already explained. In 2003 the year I was to graduate I received Christ Jesus as my personal Lord and Savior right in my room in the university. That was the beginning of a major transformation in my life. Giving my life to Jesus didn't give me instant healing; my healing did not come as a sudden miracle as I would have loved it to be. God had His own way of doing it and looking way back now I think He took me through a different road which was very necessary for me.

I am going to mention just the major episodes of the transformation as I experienced from that wonderful moment when I surrendered to Christ Jesus. First of all, insomnia did not go away but something else happened inside of me; I found a reason to live again. My hopes were restored and the vacuum and emptiness I felt within me completely disappeared. I had lost interest in a lot of meaningful things about life but God restored that part of my life. However I still could not sleep. Again the frightful pictures and the violent shakes that used to frighten me while trying to sleep disappeared as well.

All of these happened gradually. I noticed that they just dropped off as I continued to fellowship with God and other brethren in the faith. My outlook changed, though I still looked pale and sick. The important thing was the transformation that was taking place within me, gave me the enthusiasm and determination I needed to face life again. However I needed more to happen and I desired God to deal with the core issue which was my sleep deficiency.

Sometimes Jesus works things out not in our own time but in His time. I finally graduated from the university. I could sleep maximum five minutes a night. But I was very grateful considering my former absolute zero degree level of sleep. The transformation kept coming in such a way that I could hardly explain. I noticed I had completely given up every kind of hatred and resentment that I had harbored for my father and step mom. I could not understand how I had succeeded to forgive and forget the past.

I don't think any psychologist on earth would have succeeded to deal with the kind of resentment I had harbored in my heart for my father and others. I think years of prolonged psychotherapy would still have been wasted effort for any therapist because what I was going through by then was greater than myself. In addition the palpitation that accompanied insomnia began to be healed, though gradually. I am glad all of that is now a thing of the past, just like souvenirs. Thank God for Jesus, He completely healed me.

In 2006 while every one had completely left the house I picked up the famous Christian movie by Mel Gibson 'the passion of the Christ' to watch. I had watched that film before but chose to watch it again all by myself. Before watching it, I prayed to Jesus asking Him to speak to me through that movie. I just said Lord; speak to me and being such a faithful God He did speak to me. In the course of watching that film, it arrived at the point where Jesus was being beaten and bits of thorn flesh were falling off His battered body.

I was so engrossed in watching the film and then suddenly the Holy Spirit spoke to me in a clear voice. He said "see the way Jesus was beaten, do you think He can be lying that He has healed you?" immediately I put off the Television and went to the room and began celebrating and worshiping God for my total healing. From that moment I received my healing from insomnia. I can now say I have the sweetest sleep in the world right now.

I conclude here by saying that it was a horrible experience I went through, the kind no therapist on the earth could have been able to solve except Jesus Christ Himself. Of significant importance, are the lessons I learned from my grueling experience with insomnia. And the lesson is that God some times defines peoples' calling in His kingdom as a result of the particular suffering they have experienced in their life. Because of what I went through, God has been building me up for my calling which is guidance and counseling.

I now understand the predicament of other younger people who have to study through so many difficulties which their friends and others may not be able to understand. I now understand the damaging effects of divorce on children. I thank God for taking me through it and making me a testimony for His glory alone.

Evangelist St N.

CHAPTER TWO

The Father's Heart

"And God said; Let us make man in our image, after our likeness: and let them have dominion over the fish of the sea, and over the fowl of the air, and over the cattle, and over all the earth, and over every creeping thing that creepeth upon the earth. So God created man in his own image, in the image of God created he him; Male and female created he them.

And God blessed them, and God said unto them, be fruitful, and multiply, and replenish the earth, and subdue it: and have dominion over the fish of the sea and over the fowl of the air, and over every living thing that moveth upon the earth".*

THE FATHER'S HEART

The Father is the creator: He conceived the universe and brought it forth into existence through His Word. He is specialized in creation and re-creation. He that created the universe, created us all also, and out of nothing He made all that do exist. The Father makes the "nobodies to become the some bodies" He picks up individuals from nothing and makes something good out of them. He did it for me; he will do it for you.

David the shepherd boy will tell you his story. He was despised and looked upon as an unfit, irrelevant and good for nothing, except to look after the family's sheep. He was unqualified even to be counted amongst the sons of Jesse his father. He was unqualified to be counted among the men of war in Israel. But the Father in Heaven sees things differently; David was the one chosen by God to be the king of Israel. The Father turned his life and story around for good; he was chosen by the Father even though disqualified by men.

I declare today, that your story is changed for good. Those who despised and rejected you formerly will look for you. All those who deleted your name and telephone numbers from their phone book will begin to seek for means to reconnect with you. Your weaknesses will be turned to greatness in the name of Jesus Christ. Those who disqualified you in times past will come back seeking for you in humility. For the father will pour His favor on you.

The Father is specialized is recreating the stories of people who come to Him through Christ Jesus by faith. He will create a total new situation for you. He will create your world anew. I can hear Him saying, "my child, my precious child, I will make you all over again. The past will be remembered no more, because your future will be greater than your past and present". He is the potter and we are the clay. Will you allow Him today to mold you and make you after His perfect will? The Father in heaven has the best in mind for you.

I was born in a family that was shattered by the forces of the evil one, by the age of twelve I had lost my father, my junior brother and my immediate elder sister. My life was filled with bitterness, fear of death and hopelessness. My father was an alcoholic and he introduced me to strong drinks by the age of six. My future was dark and dreadful. Up to the age of fifteen I had no identification documents and no birth certificate. I was growing as a wild plant with no one to prune. And by the age of eleven I was totally bound by alcohol. But to God be all the glory, the grace of God found me on the 21st of June 1984 and changed my lifetime story. Jesus made me a new man and gave me a new reason for living.

Thanks be to God for sending His only Begotten Son to die for me. I was invited to a Gospel meeting for the first time and that night I gave my life to Jesus. My life has been recycled by God. I am a brand new creation, washed by the blood of Jesus Christ. Today I am seated with Jesus in heavenly places, He has raised me up to seat with kings and He has made me a blessing and a positive voice to my generation.

This is your season for divine uplifting. Your statuesque will changed, you are moving forward and higher and I can see you excelling in every area of your life in the mighty name of Jesus.

The Father will restructure your whole life.

Your marriage will be a new story; you are stepping into a divine new honey moon. Love and care is being restored to your marriage. Integrity and trust is being restored to your heart. I see healing taking place right now in your home. Just accept and give Him a place in your home.

The heavenly Father wants to father your marriage; will you permit Him to be your mentor and counselor? Remember, he blessed and ordained the first marriage and He will consecrate the last marriage, that of the Church and the Lamb of God, Jesus Christ the righteous.

Your Job and career will be restructured. He will reposition you for new fortunes and new opportunities. He has the whole world in His hands, and you His precious child have the first choice in life by your covenant right in Christ Jesus, for God can never give the children's meat to dogs. It is time to step into your dream job in the name of Jesus Christ. I can see you struggling with a terrible financial situation; there is hope. Just surrender to the Father's hand, all is not lost yet, all will be well for the righteous. There is always a miracle for men and women of faith.

The Father will give you the wisdom of Rahab.*

Rahab through wisdom saved her family and herself and became the great grand parent of King David and Jesus.

Your wisdom will bring total security and restoration to your entire family. You and your family will never cry when others are crying, the father will set you aside for blessings in the midst of crisis.

The Father will give you the wisdom of the Gibeonites.*

The Gibeonites by wisdom made a covenant of life and peace with the princes of Israel. They became protected by the Israelites and they lived amongst covenant people of God for life. The God of Israel became their God, the blessings of Israel become their blessings, and their enemies became the enemies of the nation of Israel. Let every covenant blessing be your portion in the name of Jesus.

May you never sign a contract that will take you down instead of taking you forward and upward in life. May you never be a victim of associating with the kind of people that will bring hardship and stress instead of peace and life. The Father will connect you with people of blessings and people that will bring fortunes to your life.

The Father will give you the wisdom of Jacob.*

Jacob by wisdom discovered the law of attraction and conception. What you see you conceive and reproduce. And he became so wealthy through the transfer of the wealth of Laban. By wisdom you will cause wealth to follow you and the wealth of the wicked will be transferred to the righteous. The foolish spends years of hard labor without wealth and prosperity.

The Father will give you the wisdom to make wealth and the wisdom to sow your seeds where there will be maximum harvest. Before you sow the next seed, find out what happened with the last seed. Did the birds pick up your seed or did it fall on thorns or on fertile soil? Learn to invest wisely and timely.

The Father will give you the wisdom of Solomon.*

Solomon by wisdom enjoyed peace, safety from all his enemies and supernatural development. He succeeded to build a historic Temple for his God in Jerusalem. By wisdom king Solomon provided answers to life's questions and during his reign the nation of Israel experienced the greatest level of prosperity and authority. He wrote more than three thousand proverbs. The wisdom of the Lord will cause you to reign over every situation that will come your way; you will never be void of answers to life's problems.

The Father will give you the wisdom of Hushai.*

Hushai by wisdom frustrated the wisdom and counsel of Ahithophel and saved King David from the hands of his enemies. Through wisdom you will frustrate the schemes of your enemies in the name of Jesus Christ. You will never be in want of insight and for wise counsel. Let the wisdom of the Father fill your mind and heart in a brand new way today. From this day you will be a fountain of divine wisdom, kings and princes will come to you for consultation and for direction in the name of Jesus.

Your wisdom will take you where money can never take you to. Doors will open to you because of divine wisdom that human connections can not open for you.

Receive the wisdom of the Father right now, in the name of Jesus Christ His Son. Ask and you will receive.

The Father will give you the wisdom of Esther.*

Esther by wisdom reversed the plans of wicked Haman. Your Haman will fail and you will be established in the kingdom. Every weapon formed against you shall not prosper.

ESTHER WAS DIVINELY CHOSEN:

She was one of the girls that were **chosen** for the contest among three thousand others. She was not rejected; you will not be rejected anymore.

Today, root out the spirit of rejection; rejection by men, rejection by your employer and even rejection by friends.

Many suffer rejection even within their close family circle. Every broken marriage somehow begins with rejection in the heart; that eventually manifest through physical and verbal separation and abuse. It is very painful to see so many children who are suffering under the yoke of parental rejection and separation. An orphan is better that a child that is hated and rejected by the parents.

You will be chosen in your family, you will be chosen in your clan. You have been chosen by God for breakthrough in this season. You have been chosen to cross over to the next year with flying colors. Your heavenly Father has chosen you for uncommon testimonies in this season believe it and accept it in the name of Jesus Christ.

ESTHER HAD DIVINE FAVOR.

She obtained favor with everybody that was placed over her. Your season of uncommon favor has come.

Divine favor will connect you to your dreamed husband or wife, for you who are still believing God for lifetime partners.

Divine favor will open the doors to your long term expectations. And no human being can close the doors that God opens for you miraculously.

Divine favor will cause you to get supernatural results that will distinguish you in every area of your life.

Divine favor is the Spirit of supernatural mercy, supernatural kindness and grace upon your life.

This is your season of favor; your heavens are opened. Step out by faith and see the difference in the name of Jesus.

Tell yourself, 'I am well favored by God and favor will flavor my days and my years. Favor will add divine beauty to my life'.

ESTHER WAS ACCEPTED BY THE KING.

The doors of the royal palace were opened to Esther and the king placed a royal crown on her head. I see you entering the place you never had thought or dreamt of before. I see uncommon doors opening up for you. You will be welcomed by princes and by kings. The nobles of your society will discover you and will come running behind you for assistance and for connections. The time has come whereby the hopes of the world have failed them and the answer is in the house of God. For Jesus is the answer to every human need.

Child of God, you are an answer to the crises around you. You are a divine provision to your world. You are born for signs and wonders; you are a solution because the grace of Jesus Christ is upon your life.

You are accepted by the Father in heaven and because heaven says yes; no man can say no. You will make it; it is not optional; it is a decree from heaven for the righteous.

Heaven has said yes to your prosperity.
Heaven has said yes to your health, for by his stripes you were healed. Every form of sickness in your body must give way.
Heaven has said yes to your certification and breakthrough.
Heaven has said yes to your advancement and promotion.
Heaven has said yes to your marriage, move forward and have no more fears in righteousness.
Heaven has said yes to the dreams of your heart, be still and see what God will do.
Tell yourself, 'I am accepted by God and it is well with me'.

ESTHER'S REQUEST WAS GRANTED.

Because of her prosperity and progress, wicked Haman secretly planned to destroy Esther and her people, but his plans failed for his wicked plans were exposed. No wicked plot against you will prosper in the name of Jesus Christ. Esther had to break protocol to make her request before the king and her request was granted by the king.

This is your season for your dream and long awaited answer to prayer. Cheer up, your request is granted and the results will soon manifest.

Your longing will be fulfilled, for the Father fulfills the longings of the righteous. Your cry will be heard, wipe your tears, your story will change and your enemy will be destroyed. The heavenly Father has granted you audience and He has the power to perform and to supply all your need.

The longing of your soul will be granted. Your dream will come to pass. Your expectation will not perish in the name of Jesus Christ. For you serve the same God as Esther, the Father did not fail Esther, the Father will not fail you, for God never fails.

Confess and declare aloud, 'nothing will destroy the dreams of my hearts. My expectations will never be frustrated. My request is granted in the mighty name of Jesus Christ'.

ESTHER'S ENEMY WAS EXPOSED AND DESTROYED.

"So they hanged Haman on the gallows that he had prepared for Mordecai. Then was the king's wrath pacified".*

Through Esther's prayers and fasting, God overturned the plans of Haman, and that which was meant for evil against the Jews turned out for their favor because God answered their prayers.

Your enemies will be exposed and defeated. The plans of 'Haman' against you and your family will never prosper in the name of Jesus Christ.

I see the destruction of the kingdom of your enemies; you will see the end of oppression and the end of captivity.

You will see the end of evil conspiracy and the end of Satanic inspired actions against your prosperity.

You will see the end of the whiles of human wickedness. The wicked is for a season but Jesus is Lord of lords and King of kings and He reigns forever and ever.

The time of the enemy's authority over your life is over, the tide is turned and the victim has become the victor. You will oppress oppression and reign over that which ruined you in times past.

This is your time to gain control over past failures and regain your momentum to live life fully in the power of redemption through Christ Jesus. Step into a brand new day.

Your enemies will become the victims says the Spirit of the living God.

Your people will be saved at last and your family will be promoted even in difficult times. Your enemies will prepare grounds for your advancement and promotion. Your temptations are just stepping stones for your testimonies and triumph. Rejoice for your enemies only work hard for your favor.

Esther and the people of Israel ended up with a great celebration.

They celebrated their victory over all the forces and schemes of their enemies. They celebrated the favor of God on their lives.

You will celebrate your healing and divine health.
You will celebrate your testimony and uncommon favor.
You will celebrate your miracle and divine intervention.
You will celebrate your uncommon wedding ceremony.
You will celebrate the birth of your miracle new born baby.
You will celebrate your family salvation and new life in Christ.
You will celebrate your citizenship.

You will celebrate your final victory and breakthrough at last.
You will celebrate your deliverance.
You will celebrate your graduation in a grand style.
You will celebrate your family reunion at last.
Your will celebrate your financial miracle in the name of Jesus.
You will celebrate your ministry's breakthrough for the glory of God. This is the set time for the manifestation of your covenant promises.

He will give you the wisdom of Nathan.*

Nathan by wisdom caused King David to see his transgression; as a result, King David humbled himself before God for salvation and forgiveness.

The Father will give you the wisdom you need to cause kings to bow down before you. You will have the grace to influence the nobles and potential people in your community for the kingdom of God in the name of Jesus Christ.

I see you struggling with guilt, conflicts, pressures and stress; the Father is an understanding Father, His grace will cleanse and purify you all over again.

Stop struggling, give it all to Him. His heart's desire is your wellbeing. All that He has belongs to you; you are the center of all His creation. Fulfill your heavenly Father's dream. Make glad the Father's heart.

Just say yes to Him today.

The Father is more than just the Creator:

HE IS THE MASTER PLANNER.

Everything in existence was in him and from him. He is saying, **"I know the thoughts I have for you… thoughts to prosper you and to give you a well planned end.***

The Coming of Jesus as our sacrificial Lamb was the plan of the Father. The Father planned your salvation well before you were created.

The plans of the Father are eternal and nothing can frustrate His plans for you. His plans are plans to prosper you and to give you a well planned future, Halleluiah.

The Father's projects for you will work out for good. He is a good Father and He has good intensions for your life. It is a blessing to know that the Father has planned our happiness for you, no matter what may come your way; it will all turn out for good.

I have made up my mind to rejoice in the Lord, my joy is a choice; my joy fulfils my Father's desire for me.

The plans of the Lord are perfect.
The plans of the Lord are eternal.
The plans of the Lord are for our wellbeing.
The plans of the enemy will not work out against you.
The plans of the wicked will not prosper against your family.
The plans of the evil one will not stand against your destiny in Jesus name.

The Father has good plans for you; begin to rejoice no matter what you may see around and about you today and right now. The Father's good will for you will surely manifest as you remain faithful to His word. Remember your Father is a loving, faithful and caring God.

Don't be shaken by what you see.
Don't be moved by the voice of the world.
Be bold and stand for the will of God for your life.
The Father's good pleasure for you will surely take you to the expected place for your life. The Father has planned your days and your years; He has programmed peace and prosperity for your years and seasons of life. He has put things in place and He has programmed testimonies and breakthroughs for the days of your life, halleluiah. The plans of men might fail but God's plans for you will surely workout well. Believe it, accept it and expect it.

Hear the word of the Lord: "your days will be good days, and your years will be filled with shouts of joy".

Trial times are for a season, tough times are but for a moment.

The things you are going through now will end up with breakthrough.

The peace and favor of the Lord is for life. You will be filled with praise and worship to the Father, for He is God.

Follow His plans, for they will work out for your good. He knows the past and the present and He has the future in his hands. Everything the Father does is for our good.

> "I thank you heavenly Father, for helping me submit myself to your perfect plan for my life; thank you from the depth of my heart, I love you".

THE FATHER IS THE DIVINE PROVIDER.
Remember the Father provided a **covering** for Adam and Eve. His will is not your shame and dishonor but your glory

and beauty. His will is not to expose you but to bring you to repentance and deliverance. The Father has provided a covering and ransom for your sins through the blood of Jesus Christ His precious and only begotten Son. Halleluiah.

The Father provided the enablement for **the Ark,** for Noah and his family. He provided Noah with the information and the skills necessary for the construction of the Ark. Noah through the grace of God was the only man saved with his family.

CONFESS THIS ALOUD:

My family will never perish with the ungodly and the unbelieving.

My family will find grace and help in times of need, in the name of Jesus Christ.

My family will be distinguished from the families of my community.

Grace will be shown to my family because of the precious blood of Jesus Christ that was shed on the cross for us.

My family will embrace the sacrificial gift of God for personal salvation and complete regeneration in the name of Jesus Christ.

My family will never be a victim in my community from this day forward in the mighty name of Jesus Christ.

God will always make a way out for me and my family in the name of Jesus Christ.

The Father has already provided for you and your family all the grace necessary for life in abundance.

You have grace for godliness and excellence. Decide to make a difference with your life through faith in Jesus Christ.

To God be all the glory: we serve the faithful provider.

The Father provided a well of living waters for Haggai and Ishmael.

> "And God opened her eyes, and she saw a well of water; and she went, and filled the bottle with water, and gave the lad drink".*

The Lord will provide for you Oasis in the desert. In times of need He will make a way for you. He will satisfy your longing soul.

The Father provided **divine insight** for Jacob.

He revealed to Jacob the law of conception through Perception and caused him to become greater than Laban his master.

Everything Jacob had multiplied supernaturally by the grace of God.

> "And Jacob took him rods of green poplar and of the hazel and chesnut tree; and pilled white strakes in them, and made the white appear which *was* in the rods. And he set the rods which he had pilled before the flocks in the gutters in the watering troughs when the flocks came to drink, that they should conceive when they came to drink.
>
> And the flocks conceived before the rods, and brought forth cattle ringstraked, speckled, and spotted".*

The Father provided a ram for Abraham in the place of Isaac. He provided a substitute for our sins.

He has paid the full price for all your guilt and pain, lift up your eyes onto Jesus Christ our Savior and Lord.

> "And Abraham lifted up his eyes, and looked, and behold behind him a ram caught in a thicket by his horns: and Abraham went and took the ram, and offered him up for a burnt offering in the stead of his son".*

The Father provided a wife fo Isaac by divine providence and leadership. The God of Abraham answered the prayer of Eliezer and led him to Rebekah daughter of Bethuel who became the wife for Isaac. God blessed their marriage with twins. The God who did it for Isaac and for Rebekah will do it for you; you will find the sweetheart of your life and be blessed with wise children.

The God who blessed them with twins will open your womb and give you kingly seeds, sons and daughters that will influence the world positively and godly in the name of Jesus Christ. Have no more fears and confusion; trust the Father for your God given lifetime partner. Your family will flourish like the family of Isaac. Your family will be marked by divine favor and grace. Let the light of God shine on you and on your sons and daughter.

He provided manna for the children of Israel for forty long years while they were in the wilderness. Your heavenly supply line will not be stopped in the name of Jesus. The Father will supply to you much more than manna; but all that will make life meaningful and reasonable. All that will make your life peaceful and happy: the Father will supply to you all that will make your life productive and resourceful.

What is the longing of your soul?
What is the dream of your life?
What is your greatest request?

What is that thing that is weighing you down?
What is that particular lack that has ruined your reputation and reduced you to nothing?
My dear friend; all is not lost yet, the end has not come yet, there is a loving Father, our heavenly Father; He will do it for you and only God has the final say over your life, so fear not.

For King David the Father provided skills and grace to kill Goliath. For Solomon the Father provided wisdom and uncommon wealth.

For Daniel the Father provided the gift of revelation and interpretation of dreams. We serve the same God and we believe in the same God. We can have the same results. Have faith to receive all that the Father has already released to your account. He has already provided all that we would ever be in need of through the life and death of Jesus Christ on the cross for our redemption. It is our responsibility to receive what we need; life, peace, victory and all testimonies were released to us on Calvary.

Remember:

The Father was the deliverer of the nation of Israel from the bondage of Egypt. He is a man of war who saved the nation of Israel from all their battles. He will fight your battles and you will see the salvation of the Lord.

The Father's heart is filled with love and compassion. He will never give you up. Never lose your faith, for God will never fail those who trust in Him. The Father cares for all that concerns you. Remain in Him and you will soon celebrate. Halleluiah.

MEDITATION.

The Story of Miss Tita

I was born November 15th and the fifth among many siblings. I am presently an orphan but had lived like an orphan even when my parents were alive. That is to say, my father divorced my mother when I was just three years of age. As a result of the divorce, I had to stay under the care of my father because I loved him.

At the age of five, my father registered me in class one primary school. When my mother came to take me away from him, I refused because I loved my father. When I was promoted to class two, my father got married to a second wife and a year later she gave birth. I was therefore taken out from school to take care of my step mother's baby. This was very painful for me, but I had no choice. At home I was treated like a slave by my step mother.

Meanwhile, I could not really feel the impact since my grandmother was still alive then, and would stop by with some things I needed. When the baby turned one year old, I had to continue school again, since grandmother could now stay with the child. By this time my father's first son left the house to an unknown destination. And at the same time my elder sister purchased my first pair of shoes at the age of ten, but they got stolen the following day. I was greatly saddened within me.

I was compelled to pick coffee from my father's coffee farm, to earn some money as a reward for the labor which I used to buy another pair of slippers. When grandmother died my elder sister was also forced to leave the compound to stay with a man they decided to be her husband. With this, she also left the compound to an unknown destination. This meant that I was the only person left to stay with my father.

Since I was the only child left in the house I had to do every farm work and the house work alone. I had to go for wine tapping, carrying wine and accompanying my father to occasions like death celebrations and traditional meetings etc. As I was left alone with him, he used to say he would not allow me to get married and I will continue to stay with him, since he has also sent the second wife away.

My father began forcing me to go to bed with him, he would promise me money just to convince me to have sex with him. When I was in class four, he sent me to stay with one woman although I did not know her. He gave his reasons for keeping me with this woman, that he borrowed some money from this woman, and used it for my brother to learn a trade so that when I will grow up, I will be married to that woman's son as compensation for the money. During my stay with this woman, I was always asking her, "will I not continue school" and she would tell me 'you will but not now' while taking me to the farm everyday.

One day, this woman and her husband brought some palm wine that I should carry the wine and follow them to my father's compound. There we met one of my cousins from a near by village. My father put some of the wine in his cup, drank and gave me some to drink. After he had forced me to drink, he asked me to give that same cup of wine to the husband of the woman I was living with at that time. When he had also drank, my father then announced to me, "that is your husband from today". I was shocked, confused and speechless. From there they forced me back home.

A month later, my father called us again, when we arrived his house he told this my supposed husband to go and bring seven bags of salt, seven gallons of oil and a certain amount of money so that they can take it to the "Kwehfor", the king makers for them to purify me traditionally. And he said if they people do not wash me ceremonially according to their tradition, then I will never put to birth successfully. With this I escaped from that woman and her husband to a near by village to meet one of my paternal aunt.

As I continued my stay with my aunt, I went to the farm everyday with her, while her children went to school and I was also responsible for all house duties.

One day I got the courage to ask her for money for my school fees, surprisingly she showed me a piece of land, and asked me to plan some cassava there and to harvest and sell for my fees. These were her words; "This land was meant to cultivate cassava, plant your cassava there, harvest them, sell and then pay your fees". This aunt of mine had an elderly son who was carrying palm wine for payment to Santa village everyday. For me to make life easy on my part, I decided to carry palm wine with him. When I carried three jugs for him for free, I would then carry two for payment; this was twenty five litters of wine for over ten kilometers on my head. I had to do this because I wanted to raise some money for my books and for some of my school needs before the cassava could get ready.

One day on my way to Santa village, with the 25 litters of palm wine on my head, I had high fever; I did not find it easy returning home. At home, I was sick for a very long period, nobody even thought of buying medications for me. It was when people from the neighborhood saw that I was close to death that they had to force my aunt to take me to the hospital. Because of the pressure, she pleaded with a certain man passing by on a motorcycle to help carry me. The man had to use a loin to tie me on his back before taking me to the health center. I was there for two weeks before recovering. While still at the health center my aunt came with a message for me, "one young man has proposed paying your hospital bills on the conditions of getting married to you in the future when you grow up". When I refused her proposal, she went ahead and sold the cassava farm which I was planning to sell and use the money for my school fees.

When I had recovered, I went to the market one day and by chance, I met my elder sister who had escape from home for several years. I asked her to give me some money for my school fees. She responded that she had settled in a certain village so I should come and stay with her and continue my education. When I got there, she bought for me some exercise books, uniforms and gave me the registration fees. I was the happiest child on earth that day but my joy was soon turned unto sadness. I could not stay with her peacefully because of so much disagreement. I had to struggle for myself to complete school fees.

While in school I had to work odd jobs each day after school just to raise some money for my personal needs. At home with my sister, I had persistent struggles with her, because of so many men that were coming to the house, my sister wanted me to follow her in prostitution, I was forced to leave the house because I refused to consent to her immoral ways. It was at this point in time that I was forced to assumed full responsibilities for myself.

I will spend the night in the cold with my dresses on my chest. With all these hardship; I had to join friends, bad friends who gave me all sorts of advice and I finally ended up raped and abused. At a point in time I came to realize that I was pregnant and had no way to go. At a certain time, my brother got the information about my sufferings and he came and saw the hardship I have been going through. He took me to one other village and left me with another maternal aunt. By this time hardship has become part of me, I was ready to face whatever came my way. Thank God I had safe delivery.

Today I am 23 and have gone through all sorts of disappointments from parents, family members and from friends but by the help of Jesus Christ I am seating for the G.C.E, O Levels this school year.

The good news is that Jesus Christ has given me peace and happiness since the day I received him as my personal Lord and Savior. I am washed by the blood of Jesus Christ and am happy and stress free. I have made up my mind to continue with my education, I want to be able to defend the rights of children and to ensure that all children have fair treatment. And by the grace of God I will make it. Together let us help give a smile to a depressed child.

Tita*

Not real name.

CHAPTER THREE

The Passion of the Son

"For unto us a child is born, unto us a son is given: and the government shall be upon his shoulder: and his name shall be called Wonderful, Counselor, The mighty God, The everlasting Father, The Prince of Peace. Of the increase of *his* government and peace *there shall be* no end, upon the throne of David, and upon his kingdom, to order it, and to establish it with judgment and with justice from henceforth even for ever. The zeal of the LORD of hosts will perform this".*

THE PASSION OF THE SON

Why Jesus is different.

The following scriptures deal with the issue of the person of Jesus Christ.

You cannot fully understand his passion until you know by revelation the person of Jesus Christ the Son of God.

Read these verses prayerfully.
"For in him dwelleth all the fullness of the Godhead bodily. And ye are complete in him, which is the head of all principality and power".*

"And the Word was made flesh, and dwelt among us and we beheld his glory, the glory as of the only begotten of the Father, full of grace and truth".*

"For he whom God hath sent speaketh the words of God: for God giveth not the Spirit by measure unto him".*

"In whom the god of this world hath blinded the minds of them which believe not, lest the light of the glorious gospel of Christ, who is the image of God, should shine unto them".*

"Who is the image of the invisible God, the firstborn of every creature".*

"Who being the brightness of *his* glory, and the express image of his Person, and upholding all things by the word of his power, when he had by himself purged our sins, sat down on the right hand of the Majesty on high".*

"But we preach Christ crucified, unto the Jews a stumbling block, and unto the Greeks foolishness;
But unto them which are called, both Jews and Greeks, Christ the power of God, and the wisdom of God".*

"Then spake Jesus again unto them, saying, I am the light of the world: he that followeth me shall not walk in darkness, but shall have the light of life.*
"As long as I am in the world, I am the light of the world".*
"Jesus said unto her, I am the resurrection, and the life: he that believeth in me, though he were dead, yet shall he live".*

THE PASSION OF JESUS

HE CAME TO FULFILL PROPHECY.

He came to cause prophecies and promises to become fulfillments and testimonies.
Everything about Jesus Christ fulfilled prophecy.
His conception as the seed of the woman was declared by God himself. God said to the serpent, "And I will put enmity between thee and the woman, and between thy seed and her seed; it shall bruise thy head, and thou shalt bruise his heel".*
His virgin birth was prophesied by Isaiah, for Isaiah declared; "Therefore the Lord himself shall give you a sign; Behold, a virgin shall conceive, and bear a son, and shall call his name Immanuel.*

His sinless life was prophesied in this manner, "He was oppressed, and he was afflicted, yet he opened not his mouth: he is brought as a lamb to the slaughter, and as a sheep before her shearers is dumb, so he opened not his mouth. He was taken from prison and from judgment: and who shall declare

his generation? For he was cut off out of the land of the living: for the transgression of my people was he stricken.
And he made his grave with the wicked and with the rich in his death; because he had done no violence, neither *was any* deceit in his mouth".*

His rejection and crucifixion, his death on the cross and his burial and resurrection all these fulfilled prophecies.

He has the power to fulfill the prophecies concerning your life and future.

There is a word and a divine promise for your life, that word will come to pass.

Abraham had a word for his life, it came to pass and Sarah smiled even in her old age.

Isaac had a word for his life and it came to pass and Rebeckah his wife gave birth to twins.

Jacob had a word for his life and it came to pass and he became the father of the twelve tribes of Israel.

Joseph had a word for his life and it came to pass and he became a prime minister in Egypt and became the source of blessing for his entire family.

David had a word for his life and it came to pass, he became the king of Israel and the ancestor of Jesus Christ.

Hannah had a word for her life and it came to pass, she became the blessed mother of Samson the Judge and deliverer of Israel. Benny Hinn had a word for his life and it came to pass, today he is an instrument in the hand of the Lord for world wide revival. Through his crusades millions around the world have found Jesus Christ as their personal Lord and Savior and received healing from their infirmities.

T.D Jakes had a word for his life and it came to pass, and he through the Holy Spirit is transforming and building the lives of millions through the Potter's house.
President Obama had a word for his life and it came to pass, today he is leading the greatest nation on planet earth: whoever thought of a black president in the United Sates of America, but God did it.
David Oyedepo of Winners Chapel had a word for his life, today he is the Pastor of one of the largest ministries in the world.

I had a word for my life and ministry and it is being unfolded day by day. Today I am the senior pastor of the World Vision International Worship Center, in Beltsville MD with several outreach programs in Africa and around the world. I see the faithfulness of Jesus Christ day by day. Everything else can fail but God's word stands sure forever and ever.

Put your name on the list. Your word will come to pass.
The prophecy concerning your future must come to pass.
The promises of God for your life will surely come to pass.
The devil cannot stop your future; the enemy cannot stop God's prophetic word for your life. Sickness cannot stop your destiny and People cannot stop your prophecy.
Even poverty will not stop your prophecy for God's word cannot be limited by any force of the enemy. Your God will break every barrier and remove every obstacle on your way.

Shout my word will come to pass.
On the Cross Jesus Christ nailed all the obstacles to your life and hindrance to your destiny and proclaimed your year of jubilee. Begin to celebrate the word of God for your life.

It is His heart's desire and passion to see you stand up by faith in His word and with confidence and assurance, knowing that His heart's desire is to see His word and covenant fulfill in your life. Jesus' dream is to see you become what the word says concerning you. He has a word concerning our career. He will guide you into His plan and purpose for your life. He has a word regarding your education and your sponsorship.

He wants to see you doing well at your job.
His passion is happy married life for you. His passion is for your children to be raised up in a peaceful and saved environment. Strife and conflicts in the family break His heart. He has deep interest to see you succeed as an individual and in the area of your calling.

Remember: your concerns are his concerns. His heart is for your salvation and wholeness. Your peace and life is His will and He wants you to live a pleasant and happy life in Him.
Remember his blood was shed for your salvation. His passion is to see you make it in life as a child of God. Breakthrough in life and success is His heart's desire for you. You need to be in agreement with His will for your life and become your dream. Let His purpose for your life, become your dream; seek to be conformed to his covenant word for your life.

Stand up and begin to confess aloud:
"My Rhema word will come to pass.
My prophecy will be fulfilled.
My covenant word will manifest.
Nothing can stop my prophecy.
In the name of Jesus Christ I will celebrate the answer to my prayers".

Hold on to the word for your life.
Your future will be a fulfillment of a personal prophecy and Rhema.

Jesus came with a passion and mission for transformation.
He did not come to conform unto the world system.
He did not come to do repairs and renovation work.
His heart is for your total transformation. His heart is to make brand new creation through his blood. In Christ we are new creatures, not renewed creature. I am a brand new man in Christ Jesus by grace.

You need to accept the fact that He is able to transform your life completely and for good. It is His heart's desire to transform your present situation and condition.
Remember: He turned darkness into light. The years of pain and guilt can be totally wiped away through his mercy and grace. It's time to let go of your yesterday and focus on today, let your today create your tomorrow.

His word is the only hope for positive community transformation; our communities are getting crazy, ravaged with crime and violence. It will take his word to see the people around us changed and be transformed from being a threat into becoming a blessing to the community.

His passion is to see your condition changed for good through your faith in His word. He did it for Hannah. He did it for Joseph. He did it for Daniel. He did it for Esther. He did it for King David. He did it for Mary Magdalene. He did it for Zaccheaus. He did it for Matthew the tax collector.

He will do it for you. Keep telling yourself, "my God will do it for me".

Think about your business situation; His grace is available for a brand new business platform and opportunity. His grace will connect you with uncommon business partners that will open to you new doors.

Consider your financial situation; He is the God of all silver and gold. He will cause you to rise above your widest imaginations. I pray right now for the grace and divine financial ideas to rest upon you in the name of Jesus Christ. Financial struggles will become a thing of the past.

Meditate on your marital situation and statues. Jesus is the source of every good husband and wife. He will give you a home and not just a house. He will give you children that will cause you to smile and to dance for joy. Today, I hear the Lord saying, "I will bring them back, all your sons and daughters that have become a curse in society" Jesus will take away all your heart aches because of his mercy and grace.

Your educational concerns, concern him. He cares for your academic success. I speak and pray for your brilliant performance right now. You will go through your course work with little difficulties for the Lord is with you to instruct and to guide you through. As you work hard, he will reward your hard work with excellence. The Lord is in need of kingdom intellectuals who will through the Holy Spirit be divinely positioned in various administrative offices for kingdom advancement. Men and women that will influence the world economically, men and women that will bring hope politically.

Your spiritual life and personal relationship with him is His greatest concern for you. These are His words, "But seek ye first the kingdom of God, and his righteousness; and all these things shall be added unto you". Let your love for God be above all other cravings. Build up your personal relationship with Jesus. Build up a personal prayer and Bible study plan. Build up your relationship with your place of fellowship. Never neglect your services in the house of the Lord. Live for Christ and you will live happy, fulfilled and peaceful.

Jesus is health; your health situation is of utmost importance.
His blood was shed for our infirmities. He is the Lord that heals us. Eat well, sleep well and play well. Exercise and keep your mind at rest. Don't store waste products in your heart, release and forgive, keep your mind free from stress and pain.

He wants to take pain and heart breaks from your life.

He has the power to turn things around for you; if only you can accept and permit him to fulfill his heart's desire in your life, for your own good. Let Jesus be your personal mentor and coach.

Accept Jesus Christ as your Lord and personal Savior today.
Pray this prayer: Lord Jesus Christ, come into my heart. I have sinned and committed wickedness, have mercy on me and forgive all my sins. I give my heart and life to you today.

Thank you Jesus Christ for coming into my life. Amen.

Jesus Christ came with a mission of restoration.
His passion is to see that you regain all that mankind lost through sin, unbelief and ignorance.

YOU NEED TO HAVE FAITH FOR:

Total restoration of abundant favor and grace.
Total and complete restoration of all that the enemy stole from you in times of sin and ignorance.

He will bring back the blessings.
He will bring back the wasted years and make your life worth living. He will restore your wisdom and understanding.

He will restore your opportunities and privileges.
He will restore your intimacy with the Holy Spirit.
He will restore your broken heart and broken live.
He will bring back joy and beauty to your life again.
He will bring back your children, who have gone astray. He wants to fix it all over again. He will bring back your finances and wealth. He will do it for you because you believe in his word. This is your season of complete restoration.
The passion of Jesus is to see you smile and dance again.
He will fill your life with beauty and praise for his own glory.
All these he accomplished for you on Calvary.

He came to seek and to save that which was lost.
His heart is for souls, lost Souls. He gave his life just for this reason. There are only two classes of people on earth; the saved and the lost. He wants to see you saved from the power of sin and death. His longing is to see you saved from the life of shame and abuse. His longing is to see you saved from all forms of defeat and failures. He longs to save you from all forms of sin and moral deficiency.
He will save your life from the danger of hell as you keep your faith alive in him.

He is our Lord and Savior.
You can be saved from all forms of initiations and satanic covenants. You can be saved from every form of demonic attacks. All these depend on your acceptance, accepting the finished

work of Jesus Christ on the cross. Call unto Him today and He will show you great and mighty things.

He came to destroy the works of the devil.
I declare that the blood of Jesus Christ that was shed on the cross has the power to set us free indeed. No more life of addictions and hopelessness. No more living under pain and heart-break and no more negative influence over your life.
Your life will no longer be ruled by fear of danger. Evil and the devil are now under your feet.
You are called to be an agent for positive change through the Gospel of Jesus Christ.

He came to produce world changers and godly history makers.
Instead of hate, love.
Instead of revenge, forgive and move forward.
Instead of bitterness, show mercy.
Instead of separation, reconcile for His name's sake.
Decide to give the enemy no opportunity to make use of you.

Jesus Christ came to empower a people for his Kingdom.
Jesus wants to see you full of his glory and power. He wants you to carry his Anointing for his kingdom building. It will take his power in you for you to better represent God's kingdom in the world around you.
Jesus wants to work in and through your life today; just yield to him.

Meditation

Jesus Christ saves and protects

It was on the 5th of May, as we were driving for a wedding ceremony; my wife, my one month old daughter, and a brother in the Lord and I where in the car. Before we left the house that morning we had some time of prayers to commit the trip into the hands of the Lord because the state of the road was terrible. Just few minutes from the city we were faced with a problem of two cars driving very swift to over take us in the second and third position. Not knowing what to do because of the size of the road, I tried to drive as careful as possible and then not knowing what happened next; I only realized that the vehicle I was driving was now positioned horizontally on the road. I turned to the brother who was with me in the car and said to him; "it looks like we have had an accident" and he said "sure".

During that time, we were still bound on our seats with seat belts. Having gained some consciousness, I asked Salomon my friend in the car: "where is my wife and the baby?" not really aware of what had happened. I latter on noticed that we were involved in a ghastly motor accident. The vehicle was seriously twisted from the front to the back. The rear windshield was shattered and the back seats where my wife and baby were seating were empty. What a drama! What a test! Salomon and I managed to leave the vehicle in search for my wife and child. One of the things that surprised me was that, during this time no other car came on the road and this was on a Saturday when traffic is usually very heavy on that high way.

As we continued the search, we latter found my wife in a gutter beside the road about fifty meters from the car. At this stage I thought the shock might have caused her to go out of the car unknowingly. How else did she get out of the car since all the doors were tightly closed; unless the Angels of God had carried her and the baby out of the car. A lot of thoughts crossed my mind but one thing was sure God himself was at work.

Having found my wife lying on the pavement we started looking for the baby. After a good search, I found her in the bush closed to the gutter where I had found my wife. At first sight, I was frightened in my heart and thought the baby was dead. As a result of that, I first held the child by the feet and thereafter I took her in my arms. But the child had her eyes closed and after observing her for some seconds, I thought the baby was dead because there was no sign of life in her.

I thought I was carrying a corpse in my hands. I shook her with fright and she opened her eyes. After all medical and radiological examinations in three different medical centres the results showed no fracture: My wife was feeling some pains because of some minor bruises which she sustained and the baby whose name is Danielle Lagloire was perfectly sound.

God made a way for my wife and the baby through the back windshield while the car was hit on both sides during the accident. They fell out of the car through the back windshield and in perfect condition, isn't that incredible; Jesus takes care of his children. He is my family protection. He is my life insurance. Great was our astonishment and all those who followed the drama were greatly amazed and gave all the glory to God for divine security. Some observers said, they knew that nobody would come out alive, but all of us came out alive and with no major injury.

To God be the glory through out all eternity.

Believe him for your security, it's all free. No monthly charges. Read Ps 91.

Léonard and Family

CHAPTER FOUR
Fulfilling Your Dream

"And Jabez was more honorable than his brethren: and his Mother called his name Jabez, saying, because I bare him with sorrow. And Jabez called on the God of Israel, saying, Oh that thou wouldest bless me indeed, and enlarge my coast, and that thine hand might be with me, and that thou wouldest keep me from evil, that it may not grieve me! And God granted him that which he requested".*

FULFILLING YOUR DREAM

I was born the sixth child of a family of seven. Born in the village of Babong and my date of birth being the 5th of June, I had my first birthday celebration on my forty first birthdays, in the town of Paderborn Germany. My Dear father was a hard working man and he believed in rewarding hard work. He had several hundred acres of Cocoa and coffee farms.
He was a man that did not believe in looking up to others for help; he did everything to be a source of help instead. He believed in being a blessing and never a burden.

He used to say, "Never say you are tired while you have not accomplished and realized the purpose for your day". As a child, my father taught me to always do my assignment before going to bed. And through out my school years this principle helped me and I graduated with excellence.

Be committed to doing your assignment, Becoming your dream is a task, a duty and an obligation. In some African tribes it is a shame and a curse to die with an uncompleted building project. So when their parents die with incomplete house project, the family members must complete the building before the burial. You must do everything in your power by the grace of God to accomplish your task and realize your goals in life. I will show you how in the following chapters.

My father's heart desire was to fulfill his dream for my life. Several times he would call me into his bed room just to let me know his plans and his expectations concerning my future. As a child, my greatest days were days when my father, would call for me, just to tell me some of his plans for me when I grow up. I remember when I succeeded for the entrance examination into Government Technical College, in September of 1980; he made a personal promise to sponsor me as far as possible with the clause that I had to succeed in my exams. This was an unusual promise, for my father had not sponsored any of my five senior brothers or sister to any school beyond the elementary or primary school level.

I was the happiest student on my first day in secondary school; at last I was a student. After three and the half months in school we had our first term holidays, and my results were good. I went to the village to meet my father and to spend Christmas with him; but my joy and celebration quickly turned into pain and frustration.

This was the holidays that changed me from within; this was the season that I cried for days but without tears. This was the season I asked God a thousand questions in one day. A few days before Christmas, my father felt ill and died on the 20th of December.

His dreams for me died with him. His plans, both known and unknown perished when he died. I was still a young boy of above twelve years of age and my light was turned into darkness, my wine was mixed with water and my gold turned into dross. Life lost its meaning and my future was covered with clouds.

My father could not fulfill his dream for my life.
Have you been through a frustrating situation?
Has the dream of your business partners for you perished through an untimely death and unpredictable circumstances of life?

Have the dreams of a trusted friend of yours, failed just too close to its realization?
Have the dreams of your husband or wife, just been shattered and your whole future, now uncertain?
Have the dreams of your fiancé been frustrated due to unwanted circumstances?

All is not lost yet, miracles still happen. Hope and divine help is still on the way through Christ Jesus.

With my dad's death, my mother took over the battle to fulfill her own dreams for my life, but the challenges of financial limitations quickly overcame her and buried her dreams. Every promise and proposal she would bring up ended with a but… She needed someone to take care of her instead of her taking care of someone due to poverty and her constant ill health as a result of her many long years of hard work, improper diet and painful living.

As you can see, my mother's dream could never come to fruition in my life. She died while I was still struggling with life. By the special grace of God my senior sister took courage to take the charge for my education. She had never entered the four walls of a classroom because our dad refused to pay her fees, since she was a female child. My dad and his friends believed that the female children were good only for marriage and for child bearing. Therefore he did not send any of the female children to school.

May God forgive their generation and ignorance? But my sister helped me through my secondary school and I finally graduated with a diploma in mechanical engineering.

But my sister's dreams and expectations failed, her dream was for me to continue with mechanical engineering and to go through the university and then get a good gob and earn some big salary. The news that the Lord had called me to serve Him full time in ministry was a hard pill for her to swallow. It all happened after she had given money through my elder brother for my admissions into Polytechnic for a higher diploma.

My dear friend, are you down cast because your dreams for your friend, a loved one or even your children have been washed away by the waves of uncertainty and the unexpected? There are so many lessons to learn in life, man's ways are not God's ways. Man's best might not be God's choice. Your dream may not be God's way of life for you. And your dreams may not be God's best for your future.

In the year 1987 God put a dream in my heart; a dream that cost me everything. This was in a small Town in West Africa. God sent Rev John Trehene to Cameroon as a missionary from the Assemblies U.S.A. He was the director of a Bible school in one of the towns in the North West of Cameroon. That great evening in the convention as he ministered, it seemed as if every word he spoke was just for me. I heard God speaking through him, and asking me to lay down my technology and pick up the Bible. It was very difficult for me to say yes to the will of God and for full time ministry; it took me almost twelve months to finally say yes to the voice of God and to decide to go to the Bible institute for ministerial training.

Today it's already twenty two years, since I said that definite yes to God and for full time ministerial calling. God's dream for me is being fulfilled and I am happy about it.

I have a dream, God put his dream in me; He put His burden within me. He has deposited his passion in me and He has put his kingdom concerns within me. God's dream has become my dream. His dream is love, his dream is the happiness of every living being and his dream is the salvation of the world. His dream is your wellbeing.

MY DREAM.

My heart's desire and passion is to reach individuals, Villages and Cities with the Gospel as the power of God for salvation. I have been preaching the Gospel of the kingdom since 1984 and every day of my life the burden for souls, lost souls, souls on the way to hell, souls sick and in bondage because of ignorance of the truth, the burden for their salvation and healing overwhelms my heart. My heart breaks every day as I walk among my people and see the suffering because of sin and a lifestyle without Christ.
Through the World Vision Gospel Outreach Ministries, I seek daily to see this dream of uncommon harvest of souls and my God is doing it daily.

I have a dream to assist the local churches and ministries in sponsoring outreach Gospel crusade programs.
Many of these young ministries have a great zeal to reach out for souls in their communities but they lack equipments and the finances for effective evangelistic programs.
My heart's desire is to respond to these areas of need for the strengthening of the evangelistic arm of local church and ministries.

Today, it's more than just a dream, I have taken steps to see it fulfilled though in a small way, but I am praying to see this fully accomplish.

My vision is the welfare of children in some of our developing countries. My heart pains as I walk through the villages around some of the communities I visit during my oversea crusade trips; I see precious children that have to take care of themselves. I see children sick and hungry and have no one to care for them.
I see children abused and rejected.
I see children abandoned on the street and in garbage heaps.
I see children who are willing to attend school and have no one to pay their tuition and fees.
My heart aches greatly when I see children roaming the street at night and with no place to sleep and with no one caring for them. I hate to see a crying child, many children are crying because of hunger. These are children, precious gifts from God but many of them are going through hellish situations on earth for reasons beyond their imagination.

My heart's desire is to integrate orphans with families and sponsor them through the home units. The dormitory type of orphanages is not healthy for these precious children today; they grow without parental guidance and care. It is a great blessing to sponsor these children through families; they grow in a family unit and have parents that love and care for them.

I have a great burden to assist needy children and street children with basic life necessities, food, clothing and medical assistance. We are putting things in place to provide rescue missions, in order to save abused children.

We are praying for grace to assist HIV/AIDS children with the provision necessary for their up keep. Many of these children die because of lack of proper food and lack of necessary medical attention.

Our offices do assist with counseling for the total restoration, healing and prevention.

We are engaged to run primary schools for rural community children. It pains me to see children of school age roaming the streets during school hours, just because they have been sent off school for lack of school fees.

"Quality education is the gateway to a better future."

Remember:
Every child needs love.
Every child needs parental care, attention and provision.
Every child needs training, quality education and guidance.
Every child needs protection and discipline for moral and spiritual development.
Every child needs the knowledge of the Word of God.
Every child needs prayers and how to pray to the heavenly Father through Jesus Christ our Savoir.
Every child needs encouragement and motivation.

God has ignited in my heart the burden to provide school fees to orphans and to grant scholarships to neglected and abused children. I visited a school in the Village of Babong that is in West Africa; many children have no school bags and basically attend classes with a few torn exercise books.

And because their parents cannot afford the school fees, these children are often driven away from classes before or during examination. They end up wasting their years in school without any achievement and eventually drop out from school sooner or latter for street life.

I pray for God's help to fulfill my dream, and may the Lord use you to heal hearts, wipe tears and give hope through the love of Jesus Christ.

It is about time to challenge the church to worldwide missions' mentality once more. Many more new religions are invading our world and so many Christians are so indifferent and lukewarm. Many behave as if the issue of lost souls does not concern them. It is my heart's desire to see the church empowered for effective end time harvest.

"Oh Lord, bless outreach ministries around the world, that are doing all in their power to reach one hurting soul today".

There is a great need for partnership, networking and mentorship for growing ministries.

Time is running out and it seems as if we are just beginning…

By His grace, do that which he has placed in your hands and do it well for his own glory.

It is my heart's desire to challenge youths toward responsibility and accountability.

My heart's desire is to assist youths discover their God given potentials and effectively develop them, through youth forums and youth conferences, especially in third world countries.

Many of our youths need motivation in order to strengthen and encourage them keep up sound moral and social life and to enable them live crime free.

There is a great need to assist youths in counseling and mentorship.

We need effective youth ministries and ministers that can prepare our youths for effective community life.
Will you respond to the need to assist youths facing moral, spiritual and career crisis? Together we can make an impact.
Let us pray for youth counselors and ministers and pray for our youths to make wise decisions on creating a befitting future.

HOPE FOR THE WOMEN

Women, especially women in the third world countries have cried enough; through ungodly cultures, and religions that favor only men. It is time to wipe their tears and mend their broken hearts.
Together we can motivate and challenge these women for rural development and poverty alleviation.
I have a heart's desire to give micro financial assistance to single parents and widows for petit trading and self employment efforts.
To equip the women of the rural communities with information for income generating activities, through women's conferences and seminars in order to alleviate poverty and oppression of women.
We have to face the challenge to assist women struggling with HIV/AIDS. And consequently there is a great need for health counseling and disease prevention amongst rural women.

This is my life and the reason for living. My dream is being fulfilled and I am trusting Jesus to enable me and to connect me with individuals of like-mindedness.

What is your dream, what is the reason for your living? Why do you seek wealth? Why do you work hard everyday? What is the meaning for life? What will you do if you have one more day to live?

Noah lived for the building of the Ark in order to preserve life and to save his family.

Abraham lived for the birth of the nation of Israel; God's covenant people through which the Messiah and savior of the world would be born.

Moses lived as a mighty deliver of God's precious people from the hand of Pharaoh, king of Egypt. Through the mighty hand of God he brought the people of Israel from their years of captivity and led them out on their way to the Promised Land.

David lived to build a God fearing kingly lineage for the preservation of the law and temple worship of the God of Israel. And through his zeal and dedication to His God, he became the blood line of the Messiah.

Daniel lived as a state's man and an intercessor in Babylon, through prayer and fasting, he affected positive changes that resulted in the decree to rebuild Jerusalem.

It is very important to note that, no matter what dreams you may have for life; it is good to always submit our dreams to the Lord for guidance and divine intelligence. I have realized that my dreams are too small as compared to what the Lord has in mind for me. His words for you, his prophetic word for your life and the revelation of his divine purpose is just over whelming. I gladly submitted my own agenda to pursue his divine agenda for my life.

He spoke to me, that He would take me to all the continents of the world to preach His word, this was in 1996. When He spoke this word to me, my monthly income was less than fifty

dollars. I was still struggling on laying foundation for effective ministry. Today his word for my life is being fulfilled in an extra ordinary way.
Thank God for the plans of your heart, remain focused and trust Him. He will always do it in a greater and better way.

Today by the Spirit of the living God, I announce to you that His word for you will surely come to fulfillment in a great way. Your future will be a product of a fulfillment of His prophetic word for your life. Your dream should be in line with your Rhema word for life. Listen to the voice inside of you, His still small voice. He will lead you unto quiet waters and onto green pastures. The more you follow him daily and faithfully, the more you'll see the reality of the manifestation of your dreams.

CHAPTER FIVE

Recreating Your Future

"And Cain said unto the LORD, My punishment *is* greater than I can bear. Behold, thou hast driven me out this day from the face of the earth; and from thy face shall I be hid; and I shall be a fugitive and a vagabond in the earth; and it shall come to pass, *that* everyone that findeth me shall slay me. And the LORD said unto him, therefore whosoever slayeth Cain, vengeance shall be taken on him sevenfold. And the LORD set a mark upon Cain, lest any finding him should kill him".*

RECREATING YOUR FUTURE

The good news is that in Christ Jesus bended sticks can be straightened no matter how crooked they have been. God caused Aaron's dry rod to bud and to blossom.
With Christ there is no hopeless situation. In Christ there is no useless person. In Christ there is always a way out for those who are willing to take hold of the truth of His word.

Cain was sentenced to death by God for killing Abel his brother. You remember that Abel's offering was accepted and that Cain's was rejected, and because of this Cain was influenced by jealousy to kill his brother. This was a terrible crime, for he was the first human murderer. God responded to the wickedness of Cain with a series of judgments.
Because of the severity of God's pronouncement against Cain, the Bible says that Cain cried to the Lord God for mercy and grace, because the punishment was more than he could bear: and God reversed the terms of the punishment from death to life. God, instead of putting a mark of death, reversed it into a mark of life. These are the words of the Lord; "And the LORD said unto him, therefore whosoever slayeth Cain, vengeance shall be taken on him sevenfold". "And the LORD set a mark upon Cain, lest any finding him should kill".*

Cain recreated his future; he transformed his story and brought new hopes and vision for his life. The fear of death was taken away and his life was filled with hope and confidence for a better future. What a joy to live without the fear of death? So many people today in our world are dying because of the fear of death. The fear of death has caused so many people to become cowards just to save their own lives. Because of the fear of death many have given up their faith in Christ due to persecution.

Cain was sorry for his sin and cried out to God to take away the death sentence that was upon him and God granted him his request. I know you have sinned and because of your sinful past you have scars and wound in your life and spirit. Remember the scripture: "For all have sinned, and come short of the glory of God", "But the gift of God is eternal life".* Thanks be to Jesus, the story did not end with our sins, the story ends with the gift of God Jesus Christ our savoir. He came to give us a second chance, to enable us recreate our future and to rewrite our story, Amen.

You still have a chance to create a befitting future. If God could listen to the cry of a murderer, He will hear your cry for a second chance. Learning from the mistakes you made in the past, there is no more room for careless mistakes and unreasonable decisions. You don't need to use your life for adventure and experiments anymore. You need to amend your life and decide to go for the best in life. Go for gold, save your precious life from all the things that are meant to ruin you instead of building you up. Make the best use of today, go for a glorious future.

Moses had to spend forty long years under hard labor as a shepherd in Median.
"Now when Pharaoh heard this thing, he sought to slay Moses. But Moses fled from the face of Pharaoh, and dwelt in the land of Midian: and he sat down by a well".*.
Moses was a blessed young man who was fed with the best of Egypt. He grew up with no stress and no lack. He had all the servants at his disposal. He attended the best school and

graduated with the best results and was the prince of Egypt. But things changed and the prince became a servant and a refugee.

Moses lost everything he had once enjoyed; he carried nothing from Egypt, not even a change of dress. He was reduced from abundance to a beggar, from palace life to servant hood. He was in this desperate situation for forty long years. Working just for food, he was in a place of no choice. He spent his daily life moving from mountain to mountain looking for some green pasture for the flock. He had a wife that he did not pay the bride prize and children he could not provide a house for. He was living under the roof of his father in law.

Though Moses was reduced to a poor shepherd, there was a seed of greatness within him. He was not called to die in the mountains of Midian as a shepherd boy. Remember that Moses had an encounter with God that changed his life forever and recreated his future. Moses saw the burning bush, and as he walk closer and turned to see clearly; the Lord God spoke to him and this was a turning point in his story.

This is the day for a turning point in your story. This run away boy was now empowered to go back to Egypt as a mighty deliverer and as the hope for the people of Israel. His story changed, your story will change in the name of Jesus Christ. Can you see how Moses was re-established and restored to dignity and honor? You were born for an honorable life, don't settle for anything less than God's best for your life.

All that Moses did was to believe God; he believed the word of the Lord and acted upon what he heard from God. Your turn around is in believing the word of the Lord for your life. Act upon what He has instructed you. Believe it, confess it and walk in the light of the word of the Lord.

God did it for Moses; He wants to do it for you.

Stop looking on the long years you have labored and wasted in vain and unprofitable labor.

Stop dwelling on your actual situation, your joblessness and poor condition.

Stop looking on your past, learn from the past and create a better future.

Today, recreate your future by faith in the Word of the Lord.

Dream it, see it, speak it, reach out to it and thank God for it in the name of Jesus Christ.

Can you see how this Moses, who returned from exile become the source of hope and life for the children of Israel. He started his new life and mission at the age of eighty. He led them for forty years and through his ministry the nation had the Laws of God, the Ten Commandments. Through Moses the people of Israel had the five books of Moses and were prepared to cross over Jordan to possess the Promised Land. No human prophet will ever be greater that Moses the servant of the Lord, for through his ministry the tabernacle was built and true worship was instituted according to the heavenly pattern.

Moses returned more powerful than his former position as a prince in Pharaoh's house. He was honored and highly blessed by God. There is still hope for you to recreate you and to re-write your story in life no matter what mistakes you might have made in times past. Christ in you the hope of glory.

Rahab recreated her future through her wisdom and faith in the God of Israel. "By faith the harlot Rahab perished not with them that believed not, when she had received the spies with peace".*

"Likewise also was not Rahab the harlot justified by works, when she had received the messengers, and had sent *them* out another way"?*

"And Salmon begat Boaz of Rachab; and Boaz begat Obed of Ruth; and Obed begat Jesse".*

Could you ever imagine that Rahab the prostitute from Jericho would ever become the lineage through which Jesus the Savior of the world, the Messiah would come from? She refused to take money from the spies from Joshua and instead sought for covenant with the God of Israel. Her name Rahab meaning "wide"; as a prostitute she had room for every kind of person.

Her story and destiny was recreated, she became the wife of Salmon and the grand mother of Jesse the father of King David the ancestor of Jesus our Lord. The God we serve is able to do it for you. There is still so much ahead of you and for you. Your story can change for better even now and for the glory of God.

Rahab was beautifully wedded despite her past life, she raised up well behaved children and he family became a blessed and renowned family in Israel. You have a beautiful future imbedded in you, seek to develop the greatness in you and step forward in life for an excellent life in Christ.

I come to speak today to your life that Jesus Christ has you in His program. Can you arise and believe that there is still a future for you and a testimony for your future? Arise and change things around you through the power of the word of God and active faith in Christ. Begin to see the next level of your life and in the kingdom of God, step forward and upward. The God we serve is the faithful God, His will is your salvation and your blessings.

Esther recreated her future, as she took the bold step to register as a candidate for the contest for the new queen of Persia. You need to know that Esther lost both of her parents and was raised up by her uncle Mordecai, before more disaster affected the family. Mordecai was captured and taken as a slave to Persia.
Is there any hope for an orphan and a slave girl, in a strange pagan nation? Yes, Esther made a difference; she believed she could reverse the course of things and change the story of her family. You know, Esther became her dream the queen of Persia, the wife of king Ahasuerus.

Don't give up; take another step of faith. Esther transformed her life from a poor miserable young girl to a resourceful and lucrative individual.

I am here today to speak to you.
I see you changing.
I see you rising up.
I see you making it in an uncommon way.
I see you breaking through all spiritual and human limitations and obstacles.
I see you testifying the goodness of the Lord in your life.
If Nelson Mandela could become his dream, you will become your dream, don't quit keep holding on.
If President Obama could become his dream, yes you can.
If Christian Ronaldo could become his dream, as number one soccer player of the year, God can do it for you. See yourself becoming your dream; take that giant step today towards the goals of your life with confidence in God.

What do you want to become in life?
What steps are you taking to realize your dream?
Esther pressed on though she was a foreigner, an orphan, and in captivity; she made up her mind to recreate her future. With the help of God she became her dream. The same God that helped Esther will help you in the name of Jesus Christ.
May the favor that caused Esther to be distinguished and established be upon you and your family in the name of Jesus Christ.

Your next level depends on the next step of faith you will take towards recreating your future.
Do it prayerfully and faithfully by the power of the Holy Spirit. The God that raised up Esther from slavery to the palace will do much more for you and your family.

God will give you a connection to the husband that will cause you and your family to change for better, for you who have been praying for your dream husband. May your wife bring increase and not decrease to your life and family. May your children cause your life to be enriched and bring honor to your life in Jesus name.

God will give you the grace to be qualified and not be rejected for promotion and for your dream job.
God will give you the connection to the palace that will become a source of life and prosperity for your entire generation.
God will take you to the community and ministry that will become the spring board for your dreams to flourish and your vision to be realized.
Let the blessings that changed the story of Esther come upon you in the mighty name of Jesus Christ.

The Prodigal son recreated his future when he decided to return to the father and sought for mercy. He was welcomed and blessed by the father. While the elder brother who was at home without any vision for life ended up outside crying. The prodigal son who had wasted all the family resources and had failed in his mission in a foreign land: came to himself and recreated his future through godly decision, humility and true repentance. The decisions you make today will greatly affect your desired future, you need just a step of faith to move to your expected future. Make that life changing decision, make that move by faith and guided by divine wisdom of the Holy Spirit.

Remember:
Noah was a drunkard.
Abraham was too old.
Isaac was a daydreamer.
Jacob was a liar.
Leah was ugly.
Joseph was abused.
Moses had a stuttering problem.
Gideon was afraid.
Samson had long hair and was a womanizer.
Rahab was a prostitute.
Jeremiah and Timothy were too young.
David had an affair and was a murderer.
Elijah was suicidal.
Isaiah preached naked.
Jonah ran from God.
Naomi was a widow.
Job went bankrupt.
Peter denied Christ.
The Disciples fell asleep while praying.

Martha worried about everything.
Mary Magdalene was demon possessed.
The Samaritan woman was divorced and remarried more that five times.
Zaccheus was too small.
Paul was too religious. Etc.
All these men and women of God recreated their future through active faith and godly wisdom. They changed the course of things around them for good. You are designed for greatness and dignity; you are called to an incorruptible inheritance in Christ Jesus.

Tangible steps to recreating your future.

> "And it came to pass, that, as the people pressed upon him to hear the word of God; he stood by the lake of Gennesaret. And saw two ships standing by the lake: but the fishermen were gone out of them, and were washing *their* nets. And He entered into one of the ships, which was Simon's, and prayed him that he would thrust out a little from the land. And He sat down, and taught the people out of the ship. Now when he had left speaking, he said unto Simon, Launch out into the deep, and let down your nets for a draught.

And Simon answering said unto him, Master, we have toiled all the night, and have taken nothing: nevertheless at thy word

I will let down the net. And when they had this done, they enclosed a great multitude of fishes: and their net brake.
And they beckoned unto *their* partners, which were in the other ship, that they should come and help them. And they came, and filled both the ships, so that they began to sink.

When Simon Peter saw *it,* he fell down at Jesus' knees, saying, depart from me; for I am a sinful man, O Lord.

For he was astonished, and all that were with him, at the draught of the fishes which they had taken: And so *was* also James, and John, the sons of Zebedee, which were partners with Simon. And Jesus said unto Simon, Fear not; from henceforth thou shalt catch men".*

DIVINE INFORMATION.

The lack of divine information was the cause of the death of Kind Saul. King Saul Could not receive any answer from God, either through the prophets or through dreams, he ended up consulting a witch which resulted to his death.
Many are deformed because they are uninformed. We can see the negative impact in our society because of either the lack of adequate information or poor and wrong information.

It is evident in our schools: students are killing fellow students and teachers, schools have now become burying ground for innocent souls.
It is evident in our society: Our society is afraid of the type of youth generation it has produced, through wrong philosophies of life or poor upbringing, based upon wrong foundations and information.
You cannot do right if you have been wrongly taught.
The output is the result of the input.

What we see on our streets is what is happening in our homes. The Christian that is lacking in the word of God will never be victorious before the world and the devil.

The disciples pressed for the word of God, they longed for divine information from the mouth of Jesus.
You need a word from the throne room of heaven.
You need to hear from God if you need to do it the God way.
The lack of divine information has caused the church today to become secular and philosophical and the result is humanism. It is time you open your heart to God for wisdom and for divine insight. You can never produce the expected results without the right information.
You need the life manual for a better life; Read the Bible, hear from heaven, be connected with Jesus and hear from him. Be informed not just with human wisdom but with divine heavenly insight. A word from God can dissolve all your doubts and fears in a moment.

If you fail to be rightly informed you have chosen to be timely deformed. People perish for lack of right information. Many are dying for believing human lies and man made doctrines that can never produce the desired results. The people pressed to hear the words of life from the mouth of Jesus, they have tried the sermons of the scribes and the doctrines of the Pharisees and their wounded souls were still sick, empty and hopeless. And they came to Jesus, the messenger from heaven for fresh manna from heaven.

Your life will always resemble what you feed yourself with. You cannot feed yourself with junk and be healthy and prosperous.

Today, be blessed in the name of the Lord: be connected to heavenly wisdom and right information for all that concerns your life and well-being. Let your heavens be open for divine revelations and divine visitations. Receive the grace to be connected to the right information for your destiny in the name of Jesus Christ. Right information will enable you to go the right way and take the right decisions for the best future.

Adam and Eve suffered the loss of everything because Eve yielded to wrong information. Wrong information led them to wrong actions and the result was a lost paradise.
The nation of Israel suffered forty years wondering in the wilderness because they believed wrong information; they believed that they were as grasshoppers. Your belief system depends on the information you accept as true. Those who believe in nothing other than themselves end up becoming nothing.

I believe in Jesus as my personal Savior because of Biblical information. I am so happy I believed the right teachings and by the grace of God I am saved and washed in the blood of Jesus Christ the Son of God.
Your belief might be what is killing you. Many are trapped in occultism because they refuse to believe the word of God; they end up trapped and bound by evil spirits and human manipulations.

Whose report do you believe? What are you being fed with? I choose to feed myself with faith and the wisdom of God through the word of God. There is no higher wisdom apart from the wisdom of the Bible, the written word of God.

Don't be fed with dreams and visions; there are so many spiritualists that use dreams and visions to entangle their followers, examine everything through the word of God. They tell you the dreams they receive for you and seduce you to their own conclusions. Let God speak to you for yourself and through sound Biblical teachings.

Don't be fed with fictions and human opinions; your existence is more than an opinion. You are more than an idea; good ideas are not God's ideas. Seek for the truth and the truth is in Jesus Christ.
"You shall know the truth and the truth shall set you free". Jn 8:32. As you continue in the truth, the truth will establish you.

DIVINE POSITIONING
Jesus stood by the lake…You need to locate your God given place in life and stand on it. Wrong positioning will result to wrong performance and poor results. I learned this many years ago as a footballer; that no matter how skillful you may be, wrong positioning will greatly affect the play style and skillfulness of every player. Find your place in life and in Christ. Stop trying to be Mr. everywhere. Stand where you will excel. Seek God's grace and leadership to find your place in life.
Be positioned in your post of duty. Let the Evangelist do the work of evangelism. Let the pastor do the work of shepherding the flock. Let the singers be positioned in the choir and music ministry. Many are failing in life because they are trying to do that which they were not called for. Fulfill your gift, stand in your calling and know what you were created for, then engage yourself to do that which you were called for in life.
Develop your gift and equip yourself for excellence.

As long as you are in your place in Christ you will find grace and favor to do all that which you were called unto. It will take right positioning to be divinely connected, for as many are led by the Spirit of the Lord they are the sons of God.

Be positioned by the Holy Spirit.
Be positioned in the place of your excellence.
Be positioned where your gifts can be fully put to use for maximum impact.
Be positioned where you will grow and be a greater blessing to your community and generation.
Don't spend your years roaming about from conference to conference. Many have become conference addicts. Know what you are called to accomplish and commit your life to your divine assignment.
Seek adequate training for your assignment and commission.
Being in the wrong place in life produces death and vain labor.

"Look not upon me, because I am black, because the sun hath looked upon me: my mother's children were angry with me; they made me the keeper of the vineyards; but mine own vineyard have I not kept". Song 1:6.
It is hard to play well in a wrong position. Many are poor and tired, because they spend all their lives in the wrong business and in the wrong community of persons. It is time you reposition yourself. It is never too late to correct yourself. Listen to the voice of the Holy Spirit within you and allow Him to lead you in life, and all that concerns your success on earth. In the right place you will meet the right kind of individuals that will contribute the right kind of influence that you need for the right kind of life and mentality that you need for your next level in life.

"Father I pray that your precious child will be positioned by rivers of living waters. May your life never be planted in the wilderness but be positioned on green pastures for the fullness of grace that you need for your breakthrough in this season and always, in the name of Jesus Christ".

"Blessed *is* the man that walketh not in the counsel of the ungodly, nor standeth in the way of sinners, nor sitteth in the seat of the scornful. But his delight *is* in the law of the LORD; and in his law doth he meditate day and night.
And he shall be like a tree planted by the rivers of water, that bringeth forth his fruit in his season; his leaf also shall not wither; and whatsoever he doeth shall prosper.
The ungodly *are* not so: but *are* like the chaff which the wind driveth away. Therefore the ungodly shall not stand in the judgment, nor sinners in the congregation of the righteous. For the LORD knoweth the way of the righteous: but the way of the ungodly shall perish".*

RIGHT VISION
And he saw two ships…
We live in an age where the church has replaced vision to reasoning. The church is filled with intellectually blind Christians who have eyes but cannot see.
The questions that I want to ask you today is this?
What do you see? How do you see things? How far do you see? The world around us is filled with bad news every day; all they see is hard times, hurt, crimes and crisis. What do you see?

When Stephen was being stoned to death he saw the glory of God and Jesus standing on the right hand of God. And said; "Behold, I see the heavens opened and the Son of man standing on the right hand of God".*

Moses saw a tabernacle in heaven and was asked to make one similar to what he saw.

This is Prophet Isaiah's confession: "In the year that king Uzziah died I saw also the Lord sitting upon a throne, high and lifted up, and his train filled the temple".*

What do you see?

Confess this with me.
As for me and my family, in the name of Jesus;
I see great opportunities surrounding us.
I see uncommon favor overshadowing us.
I see open doors in all directions.
I see the wealth of the Gentiles being transferred unto my ministry.
I see the glory and power of God all over my family and ministry.

In the name of Jesus Christ:
I see your heavens open for good and for live.
I see increase and uncommon growth for all of you dear partners.
I see the Holy Spirit doing a new thing in my life and in your life and family.
I see the glory of the Lord over your business.
I see your wedding gown and wedding day glorious.
I can see your next job, filled with honor and excellence.
I see your path glowing brighter and brighter every day.
I see your miracle being manifested in an uncommon way.
I see Jesus Christ being glorified in and through your life.

You choose what to see. You have the right to walk with open eyes or with closed eyes. You choose what to focus on in life.

You define what to pursue and what to attract in life.
See beauty and peace.
See wellbeing and health.
See goodness and mercy.
See grace and glory.
See Angels and not demons.
See love and satisfaction.
See happiness and safety.
See success and promotion.
See heaven and not hell.
Create your day by what you see and by what you declare; see peace and blessings. See what God wants you to see and not satanic inspired visions. See the works and wonders of God and not the activities of the wicked. See Jesus every moment of your life.

How do you see things around you?
Change the way you see.
See rightly; see with the eyes of faith.
See with the wisdom of the word of God.
Begin to see God-given visions: and may you see the blessedness that God has pre-programmed for your life and future.
He has prepared a special table for you.
See your days and years blessed and filled with testimonies.
I see you rising up beyond human limitations.
See your life filled with glory and grace.
See yourself smiling, singing, dancing and filled with the Holy Spirit.

Never see your enemies over and above you.
Never see any challenge more than you can handle.
Never see yourself unfit and unqualified for any task.
Never see hopelessness and confusion.
Never see impossibilities and disqualification.
Never see poverty and lack, see abundance and prosperity.
Never see the devil working, see your God at work in you, through you and for you, in the name of Jesus Christ.
You need much more that secular education; you need the right vision for life in order to soar like Eagles and to be bold like the Lion.
If you see the wrong vision, you follow the wrong things and consequently you end up in the wrong place in life.

RIGHT EQUIPMENTS
He entered into one of the boats, which was Simon's…
Jesus needed the boat because of the crowd; He needed to thrust the boat a further into the sea in order for the waves to carry His voice to the huge crowd. Jesus needed the right vessel for the right purpose. You can never perform any task perfectly with wrong tools. You should know what you need in order to accomplish your God-given task and to fulfill your dream.

Choose the vessels that will produce the right and desired results. Choose your tools wisely and purposefully.
Equip yourself with the right tools.
The question today is this; are you equipped for life? Are you equipped for the dreams you carry? Are you ready to create the future you longed for? Good life is not for lazy people.
A student without books is equipped to fail.

A pastor without a study Bible and a place for personal prayers has planned to feed his church with emptiness and eventually will end up dry and unproductive.

A business man or woman without good financial system will eventually run bankrupt.

Are you equipped for the next level of your life? God has so much more for your life but he wants you to be ready and competent for all He has for you. God will never give inheritance to children, the inheritance is for grown ups. The inheritance is for sons and daughters that are well able to handle with care and responsibility, with integrity and dignity all that the father has in store for them.

Be equipped for success and wealth.

Be equipped for growth and expansion.

Be equipped with skillfulness for greater responsibility in life.

RIGHT INVESTMENTS.
He entered into one of the ships which was Simon's...
Simon invested his boat for the ministry of Jesus; the result was two boats of fish.

Every right investment is profitable and productive. The seeds you eat they die for ever and the seeds you sow on good soil they live for ever and will keep producing fruits for life. The condition of your future depends on what happens to your investments. If you fail in your investments you create a painful and struggling future.

You need to discern the right soil for investment. Your soil may be an individual, a ministry, a project, etc.

For Simon Peter, when he came to the end of the road and was washing his net to go home empty and sad, Jesus came along and gave him an opportunity that changed his entire life.

I believe that your future will be a reward of right investments. There are so many friends around the world that have been reduced to ruins because they spent all their years investing on bad soil; the result is poor harvest and vain labor. It is sad and frustrating to put in so much just to get absolutely nothing back as a reward.

Your time is an investment.
Those who wisely invest their precious time will surely get back more than a hundredfold reward. The difference between the wise and the foolish is in where and how they invest their time. Seek the Lord to help you invest your time wisely and in the right place and persons and for the right purpose.

The reward of wise time investment and management can never be over-emphasized.

Your financial investments.
You can never be successful and poor. There is no poor and satisfied and happy individual, yet so many individuals are walking down the way of poverty and lack because they refuse the counsel of the word of God. Right financial investments will take you to total financial freedom. Being debt free is possible, for it is written, "you shall lend unto many nations".* Money is a blessing and not a curse, poverty is never from God nor does it please God. God wants to see you blessed and prosperous and the way to financial breakthrough is wise financial investments. Wealth is for the wise, pray and gain wisdom for where and when to invest financially and how to go about it.

The earth if too rich for you to be poor.

Your words.
Your words can be an investment. The world is ruled by words, spoken and written words.
The words you speak can open or close doors for life.
The words you speak have life giving power. Remember God created the entire universe with spoken words. Invest your words creatively and responsibly. You close your mouth, you block your destiny. Speak reasonably, speak timely, and speak purposefully. The law of receiving from God is based on "request" He said, "ask and you shall receive", he said "whosoever calls upon the name of the Lord shall be saved".*

Your person. It is good to know that you are an investment. Your parents have invested in you; your church and pastor have invested in you. It is time for you to invest yourself in the kingdom of God. You were created to be a solution for some ones problems. Invest yourself for the salvation of souls; invest yourself for positive transformation of the world around you. Invest yourself to give hope to a child in a desperate and confused situation. We are called to serve the Lord with all our might and with all our souls and with all our ability.
Prayerfully discern where to invest your strength and energy in serving humanity. Let your life be a positive contribution to your world and to the house of God. May the Holy Spirit help you and direct your heart to invest your love and mercy in the right person, in the right projects and in the right ministry.

DIVINE PROVISION.
Peter met Jesus with his empty net and with an empty boat but he ended up with two boats of fish.
You need much more than your wages; you need divine provision for uncommon breakthrough in life. Mankind is weak and

limited and all our performance is limited to human ability and understanding. We need much more than human strength and wisdom for the dreams of our hearts to be accomplished, we need supernatural assistance and divine enabling for the unusual to become humanly possible.

I am trusting God for provision of divine strategies for the establishment of our ministry in new mission fields.
I am trusting God for divine provision of creative ideas that will cause my life and ministry to be unique and excellent in effectiveness and productiveness.
You need absolute faith in Jesus in order to become your dream and create your future. Find out what you real needs are and trust God for them. Our needs vary, based on our assignments. Understanding your assignment in life, and the task ahead of you; will give you the right information necessary as concerning the steps towards achieving the goals of your life.

Your need might be quality personnel for your organization.
Your need might be material provision, land, a building, educational needs or even financial needs. For Simon Peter, he wanted fish and he got two boats. King Solomon needed wisdom and he received wisdom and wealth. Elisha needed double portion of Elijah's anointing and his request was granted. What is your need today? If you fail to define your real need today, you have failed to define your future. You can never solve the unknown problems of life. Your future will be a reward of the problems you solve today. If you fail to solve today's problems you only save more trouble for your future. The provision you need from God will grant you the grace to live beyond human limitations, for God is our eternal source.

Have faith in God for He has the power to perform what He has promised. He will do more than our widest imagination, He is God.

DIVINE PARTNERSHIP
They beckoned unto their partners... Jesus needed Peter to partner with him in order for him to effectively address the multitude. And Peter was in need of John and James in order for him to pull out the net into the boat. You can never do it alone. Every great man or woman of God is as a result of quality God-given partners; you need men and women who understand the call of God in your life and are willing to stand with you to make it happen for the glory and advancement of the kingdom of God.

Begin today by being in partnership for the success of your father in the Lord or mentor in ministry. Sow your seeds to make it happen to the people that bless and enrich your life. God will not sponsor you unless you are willing to sponsor others in the kingdom. Remember; "they that watered shall be watered".*. Plant the tree if you want to eat the fruit. I can never over emphasize concerning the blessings I have received as a result of sowing in the ministries and lives of God's precious servants.

As a faithful partner, begin to believe for your God-sent men and women of God, men and women who have the commission to bless and support what God has placed in your hands. God will raise up people to stand with you until the vision is fulfilled in Jesus name.

You need partners for much more than financial reasons.

You need partners who can stand in the gap in prayers and intercession.

You need partners who will be available to work and to give their time sacrificially as need be.

You need partners who will contribute skillfully with their talents and gifts for the building of the ministry.

You need partners that will believe God and stand with you even when things don't seem to be going the way you would desire.

The good Lord will do it for you, you can't force things out, you simply trust and obey the Master and He will bring it to pass.

Pray for business partners that will be a bridge to your next level and that will connect you to your financial breakthrough.

MEDITATION

BREAKTHROUGH SECRETS.

Believe in yourself and have confidence that you can compete against all odds through Christ. Have a vision of what you would like to accomplish and be able to work hard for that vision.

Have faith for great opportunities: handle and manage them well with the fear and wisdom of God when they do come by. Always aim beyond the best, more than a hundred percent. Be on time; make your customers feel appreciated. Follow your passion and work hard, your breakthrough will come.

Never be afraid to ask questions, seek to know all that you need to know for the best result. Seek for the right mentor and listen and learn. Real success is for good students.

Take things one day at a time with a long term vision. Be focused on what is in front of you and do it best.

Don't be afraid of taking risks, success is the product of successful risk taking. If you have doubts about a business decision don't go for it. Follow your inner spirit.
You need to advertise what you have, invest to advertise your skills and business. You must continually market your business. Stay involved in the community you live in.

Don't allow rough times to discourage you. You have to be prepared to overcome every form of challenge.
Believe you have what it takes to come out more than conquerors.

Learn to delegate.
Stop compromising your moral values.
Stay focused on your goals.

Don't buy more than you can afford. Develop spending plan.
Be in charge, don't allow people to pull you around.
Be yourself.
Believe in change, refuse to be stagnant, keep evolving progressively. Move forward in life. Life can never be excited without change.

Maintain and develop quality. Quality is attractive.
Discover who you are in Christ and seek your satisfaction in the presence of God.
Totally dedicate yourself in your interest and trust God to make it happen in a great way.

Stay humble, do the research and be educated. Read books.
Give yourself time to learn your craft develop new skills.
Be courageous, be bold. Don't let money be the sole motivation for getting into business. Life is more than money.
Define your values.

Be consistent in what you do as long as you love it and have satisfaction in it.
Pay attention to the details. Seek to make a difference, learn from your mistakes.
Show that you know by your excellent performance. Let others know that you know and can do it better. No body will employ your skills until they know that you can do it well.

Treat people with respect and courtesy. Manifest the love of Christ.
As you give you receive, give your best to get the best result.
Recreate your future with absolute faith in the name of Jesus for your breakthrough.

CHAPTER SIX

Breaking The Cage

"*Moreover take thou up a lamentation for the princes of Israel, and say, what is thy mother? A lioness: she lay down among Lions; she nourished her whelps among young lions.*

And she brought up one of her whelps: it became a young lion, and it learned to catch the prey; it devoured men.

The nations also heard of him; he was taken in their pit, and they brought him with chains unto the land of Egypt.

Now when she saw that she had waited, and her hope was lost, then she took another of her whelps, and made him a young lion.

And he went up and down among the lions, he became a young lion, and learned to catch the prey, and devoured men. And he knew their desolate palaces, and he laid waste their cities; and the land *was desolate, and the fullness thereof, by the noise of his roaring. Then the nations set against him on every side from the provinces, and spread their net over him: he was taken in their pit. And they put him in ward in chains, and brought him to the king of Babylon: they brought him into holds, that his voice should no more be heard upon the mountains of Israel".**

BREAKING THE CAGE

The caged Lion

It is terrible to be caged. Have you ever had the experience of being trapped in an elevator due to either power failure? It is a terrible experience.

Some years ago I was caged in a police cell because I led a woman who was a church chair lady to Christ and her pastor arranged with the police to lock me up for causing the woman to change her faith. I was forced to stay in that tiny room with no windows, no toilets, and no seats, but small holes on the walls for ventilation. I truly experienced what it meant to be caged. This happened while I was preaching in Africa: in a cage your power and potentials are virtually useless.

Think of the dilemma of a caged Lion, a weak dog is better than a caged lion. The Lion was created to be the king of the forest, full of power and born to dominate. But imagine a Lion becoming the prey, captured, confined and limited.
I see people everywhere I go:
Intelligent but caged; beautiful but caged.
Some are very strong but caged, rich and still caged.

Full of potentials but caged.

I see wives and husbands that are caged.
I see children caged and in real bondage in life.
I see business men and women caged and in fear.
I see even pastors and churches that are caged false doctrines.
The caged Lion was no more in charged of his life.
The Lion had no more any will of its own; he lost the power of choice. His life was at the mercy of its captors. It was still full of power but had no way to fulfill his dreams.
All the Lion could do was to move in the same place round and round but going nowhere in life.
Can you imagine the disappointment of the Lioness? All her investment in the young lion was lost. The young Lion was to go forth and bring sustenance for the family but it ended up caged and in captivity.
The expectation of the Lioness was frustrated…
Are you disappointed about your family? It is very painful to invest in people that become a failure and a disgrace.

The Lion was caged.
The enemy's strategy is to cage individuals with great potentials. He is after your gifts and the role you were born to play in your generation. He wants you to be silent and quiet. God created you to be a blessing to the world, to impact generations. You are alive to positively change your world through Christ. You can't afford to be irrelevant and voiceless.
The enemy is not after the 'nobody's', he is after men and women that were born to be a voice, individuals that have what it takes to make their world a better place.

The enemy is after your greatness and success.

He is after your achievements and prosperity.
He is after your breakthrough and your influence in life.
He wants you to live without influence and without authority.
He wants you to live without creating impact in your community.
He wants you to live on the mercy of others.
The enemy has failed in the name of Jesus Christ the Son of God. No power of darkness will stop the dream of your life; you will fully satisfy the heart of God. And through faith in Jesus Christ and the authority of the word of God, you are more than conquerors.

Samson was caged.
"And she said, the Philistines *be* upon thee, Samson. And he awoke out of his sleep, and said, I will go out as at other times before, and shake myself. And he wist not that the LORD was departed from him. But the Philistines took him, and put out his eyes, and brought him down to Gaza, and bound him with fetters of brass; and he did grind in the prison house".*
This was Samson the Anointed of the Lord.
Samson the result of many years of prayers and intercession.
Samson the hope of Israel, their deliverer and prophet.

Samson was caged because of the love of strange women. He was attracted by the wrong kind of women. He was enticed by an ungodly and corrupt woman. Because of Delilah the man of God was bound by his enemies and his eyes were plucked out; he ended up blind and a caged and in abusive torture by his enemies the Philistines.

You see, Samson was gifted but caged. Used by God but caged. It is time you overcome the lust after strange men and women, the lust of the flesh. Whether you are married or not, you have to overcome the force of sexual immorality. This is the force that has caged so many kings and potential citizens of the kingdom. Many great men and women have been silent and reduced to history because of illegal affairs. Never allow sexual scandal to destroy your dream and rob you of your future and place in life.

Joseph was caged.
"And he put them in ward in the house of the captain of the guard, into the prison, the place where Joseph was bound".* Joseph was the son of Rachel; born after several years of childlessness. He was a treasure for Rachel and Jacob. The Bible says, "Jacob loved Joseph".* But he was beaten by his brethren and caged in a pit.
Joseph was caged because of family jealousy: Joseph was a victim of family wickedness. His brethren sought to kill him thinking that they could kill and stop his dreams. I have good news for you, you are a prophetic and covenant child and no human being or wicked spirit will succeed in killing or caging the dreams of your life in Jesus name.

Joseph was caged by the Ishmaelites.
They Ishmaelites bought Joseph and took him to the slave market in Egypt. Can you imagine the ill treatment that Joseph received from his cousins? No one showed him any mercy or kindness; they treated him as a beast, he was forced against his will; they led him to a strange land caged.

Joseph was caged by Potiphar and from Potiphar's house to the dungeons.
Joseph in Potiphar's house worked hard everyday just for food and to save his life. He could not go anywhere except working under serious supervision. The greatest fear of Potiphar was to

lose Joseph, for he discovered that everything prospered in his house under the care of Joseph. Therefore Potiphar's dream was to make Joseph a lifetime slave to work for his prosperity. He made him chief of all the slaves in his house and over all that he had.

The more useful Joseph was in Egypt the more he was caged. And in Potiphar's house Joseph became the chief among the caged and while in prison he also became a leader amongst the prisoners. Can you see how he moved from one caged situation to another? And the greatest trap that Joseph found himself in was to Marry Asenath the daughter of Potipherah priest of On. Joseph was caged with strange gods in his house.

Daniel was caged.
"Then the king commanded, and they brought Daniel, and cast *him* into the den of lions. *Now* the king spake and said unto Daniel, Thy God whom thou servest continually, he will deliver thee. And a stone was brought, and laid upon the mouth of the den; and the king sealed it with his own signet, and with the signet of his lords; that the purpose might not be changed concerning Daniel. Then the king went to his palace, and passed the night fasting: neither were instruments of music brought before him: and his sleep went from him.

Then the king arose very early in the morning, and went in haste unto the den of lions. And when he came to the den, he cried with a lamentable voice unto Daniel: *and* the king spake and said to Daniel, O Daniel, servant of the living God, is thy God, whom thou servest continually, able to deliver thee from the lions?

Then said Daniel unto the king, O king, live for ever. My God hath sent his angel and hath shut the lions' mouths, that they have not hurt me: forasmuch as before him innocency was found in me; and also before thee, O king, have I done no hurt. Then was the king exceeding glad for him, and commanded that they should take Daniel up out of the den.

So Daniel was taken up out of the den, and no manner of hurt was found upon him, because he believed in his God. And the king commanded, and they brought those men which had accused Daniel, and they cast *them* into the den of lions, them, their children, and their wives; and the lions had the mastery of them, and brake all their bones in pieces or ever they came at the bottom of the den".*

Daniel was caged because of the jealousy of his colleagues. His friends saw the wisdom and grace that Daniel possessed and decided to eliminate him. We live in a world full of jealousy and envy, even amongst brothers of the same family. The plan against Daniel failed, so shall every evil conspiracy against you fail in Jesus name.

The God of heaven, the true and living God delivered Daniel. God will deliver you from every form of Satan, cultic, cultural, spiritual or religious cage you may find yourself in today, in the mighty name of the Lord Jesus Christ.
I stand as God's servant to proclaim liberty from every form of emotional or psychological cage in the name of Jesus Christ.
I confess your year of freedom and complete deliverance.
The plan of the evil one will never succeed against you in the name of Jesus.

Some common characteristics of a caged life.

- Inexplicable misfortune.
- Being exposed to public shame, though not guilty.
- Total lack of success and advancement even though you work hard and are qualified.
- Constant struggling without achievement.
- No body delights to show you kindness; those who try to assist you end up in great difficulties.
- You cannot give account of how you spent your money no matter how much you earn; you will still be in financial hardship.
- You have suffering and sickness as a life style.
- You cannot keep a wife or husband. You are always left alone and lonely, even though you have children, none have concern for your wellbeing.
- Constant victim of disasters and afflictions.
- Miscarriages and premature death as a family custom.
- People are trained but never have a job up to their level of education.
- Mysterious death and accidents in your family.
- Intelligent and hard working but no success.
- People take delight to cheat you.
- Those who owe you refuse to pay the debts.
- You labor for others to eat, you never enjoy the fruit of your labor according to the Bible.
- People cease your property and inheritance by fraud.
- The people you've helped refuse to help you.
- You always suffer as a result of false accusations and misinformation.
- People always misunderstand you and misjudge you.

- Nothing good comes easy for you, you have to work hard for all your life, neither blessing nor favor.
- You have inner sadness without a just cause.
- Victim of spiritual obsession, oppression.

Today the cage must be broken in Jesus name.
"Our soul is escaped as a bird out of the snare of the fowlers: the snare is broken, and we are escaped".*
We break loose every form of cage in your personal life as an individual.
We break today every family cage; every power that has kept your family caged over the years is broken in the mighty name of Jesus.

Today I declare community deliverance and I declare national deliverance. I come against every force that had dominion over our nation and every force that had influenced our nation negatively in the name of Jesus. I declare the year of freedom through the blood of Jesus. Let there be peace and prosperity, let there be national revival and the restoration of justice.

Let the oppressed go free in the mighty name of Jesus Christ.
We break and denounce the cage of sin in our lives in the name of Jesus Christ the only Son of God.
We break the cage of satanic oppressions and the cage of fears and we break every bondage of soul ties in the name of Jesus.
We break the cage of family and bloodline curses, we reverse the curse and pronounce the blessing of the Lord upon your life and family.
We break the cage of poverty and joblessness in your life and community. The doors of good jobs are open for you in Jesus name.

We break the cage of singleness and lack of husband or wife.
We break the cage of divorce and pronounce the grace for peaceful and happy marriage in Jesus name.
We break the cage of misfortunes and disasters in life, no evil will come anymore near your dwelling place.
We break the cage of unbelief and godlessness in our nation in the name of Jesus. Let the light shine in your life.
Begin to rejoice and be glad in your freedom in the name of Jesus.

Meditation.

My journey to peace and freedom, By Mag

I was born in the town of Limbe, South West region of Cameroon; I am from a polygamous home where my mother was the second wife. I'm the third child of five siblings from my mother and the eleventh child of my father. I lost my father on the 14th of June 1998 and by that time I was in class six in the primary school. In addition to my father's death, I lost my twin sister when she was just above one year.

After my father's death, I became a very lonely child; I loved sitting in the dark because of sadness. My family members were sometimes very suspicious of me and thought I was possessed because I was always alone. I developed the love for Gospel meetings and I attended some when ever I had the opportunity. The only person

I could trust was God. I was asked to stay with my elder step sister, though she was not very kind to me but by the grace of God she was responsible for my school fee. Some days I went for long hours without food. During holidays I usually carried boiled groundnut and oranges from street to street on a tray to raise the money my step sister will use for my school fees and books. So many times after school we will go to the farm without haven eaten anything. The work in the farm was too tedious for me due to hunger.

I was more of a house help in my sister's house than a sister. People usually asked her even in my presence, "is this your house help"? Looking at the way I was dressed you would think that I was not a relative. Unfortunately she died when I was in the third year in secondary school. While she was alive she used to give me her children's used dresses, that was the way I got some dresses, now that she was dead things became more terrible. When someone gave me money by chance, I used it to buy some under wears for myself as a little girl. After the death of my father my mother could not help us because she was so poor; and could not afford food for us to eat. We depended on God for daily bread. That was the reason I had to be sent to live with my step sister.

I gave my life to Jesus Christ at the age of fourteen during the holidays; at this time my family did not want to hear anything about church or Jesus. Many times I was beaten just for attending church service. Many times they would take away my school bag, uniform and all my dresses as punishment for attending church against their will. Some times they will beat me around 11.00 pm and would push me outside to spend the cold night sleeping on the veranda.

And finally they pushed me to the street; they drove me from the house that I should only come back when I have denounced

Jesus and stopped church. I did not know were to go that night and by the grace of God, I decided to go and see the pastor.

By the grace of God and through the pastor's intervention, I was readmitted to the house and my dresses restored to me. Since my step sister was the person responsible for my fees, when she died nobody could afford to pay my fees. By the grace of God the church took over my education from that time until I got to form five. They also sent me to a Bible school for one year. The church could not continue to sponsor me to high school due to financial limitations.

In my family nobody cared, everyone was after his or her own individual struggles. The family only cared to meet to celebrate funerals.

But today my God has changed my story; I serve as the secretary general of the World Vision Outreach Ministry's head office in Cameroon. My heart is healed and restored. I am happy in life and my faith is established in Christ. There is no situation that is hopeless in Christ, He will do for you much more than He has done for me. My secret was daily trust and faith in the word of God. I believed that with Christ all things are possible and that He will open a door for me. To God be all the glory for the grace that I received in Christ Jesus. Faith in Jesus Christ is the real cure to stress and depression. Trust Him and lean on Him.

Mag

The cage is broken. Jesus Christ is Lord.
Let your deliverance be permanent in the name of Jesus Christ.

CHAPTER SEVEN

The Moses and the Joshua generation

"Now after the death of Moses the servant of the LORD it came to pass, that the LORD spake unto Joshua the son of Nun, Moses' minister, saying, Moses my servant is dead; now therefore arise, go over this Jordan, thou, and all this people, unto the land which I do give to them, even to the children of Israel. Every place that the sole of your foot shall tread upon; that have I given unto you, as I said unto Moses".*

THE MOSES AND THE JOSHUA GENERATION

The Moses Generation

The Moses generation was a generation of people that were raised up in slavery and oppression. They grew up with slavery mentality. They saw themselves as servants and subjects to the Egyptians. Their parents were slaves and their children were also born in slavery. Oppression and Subjection was their daily life style.

This is the way several people live their lives today; they live in oppression and subjection to their oppressors because of lack of the knowledge of the word of God and their true identity in Christ.

The Moses generation was a generation that grew up in fear and intimidation. Imagine what happens when a young Israelite sees an Egyptian some of them because of fear, look for where to hide. They saw themselves lower than the Egyptians and unable to compete in every way with them.

The Moses generation was a generation of people that knew the pain of working under task masters. Poverty and lack was their life style. They worked hard everyday just for food and nothing more.

Today there are so many people who work hard just to pay bills and have no pleasure in life any more. Life has become hard work just to survive and to sustain their existence.

This was my story, working so hard but with an empty bank account.

For several years I could not get two thousands dollars in my savings account.

It seemed as if I was working so hard just to enrich my company and at the end of the month I was more burdened and poorer than ever. It was as if I found myself in a trap; it seemed like my family and community were domed to poverty and hardship. I was raised up in the bloodline of poverty. My grandfather was poor, my father was poor and it seemed as if I had inherited the family poverty and hardship lifestyle; the Moses generation.

The Moses generation was a generation that was sentenced to death by Pharaoh. All the male children were sentenced to death from birth. Several pregnant women had to go on secret exile from Egypt before giving birth because of the desire to preserve their male children.

The Moses generation was a generation of people that were born with warfare already against their lives. The enemy hated them before they were even born, because they were children with a divine covenant.

My dear friend; no matter the circumstances surrounding your birth and childhood life, the God of Israel who saved Moses and his generation will surely save, deliver and fully restore you in the name of Jesus Christ.

The Moses generation was a generation that had female children and female youths on the streets but no male children. The enemy targeted all the potential seeds of the children of Israel, but he failed. God has a way of preserving His chosen people in times of calamity, devastation and persecution. The enemy will surely fail in your life in the name of Jesus. Have no fears, your God will always make a way for you. There will be a 'Miriam' for your life. Miriam was used by God to rescue Moses from River Nile.

The Moses generation was a generation that saw themselves as hopeless and powerless as the grasshoppers. They had no military and no weapons of war.

The Moses generation saw exile and death as the only and best way to save themselves from the bondage of Egypt. Moses fled for his life and was in exile for forty long years. He left the palace to the wilderness.

The Moses generation is that generation that cried out to God for deliverance. Because their torment came to its apex, they had no more power to bear and they cried to the Lord for salvation and for mercy.

The Moses generation was tired of the suffering and authority of Pharaoh. They believed God for freedom from the kingdom of pharaoh. The Moses generation is that generation that experienced the Passover. They saw the power of obedience and faith in the word of God. The blood upon their door posts worked, the Angel of death passed over their houses because of the blood. Faith in the blood of the lamb made a difference in the land; those without the blood lost their first born.

Today the blood of the Lamb of God, Jesus Christ the Son of God is the only true source of security and deliverance from the Angel of destruction. Nothing can hide us from the judgment of God except faith in the sacrificial blood of Jesus Christ that was shed on Calvary. Apply the Blood of Jesus today upon your life, have faith in the blood of Jesus for your total peace and safety in this troubled world.

The Moses generation had the Passover from Egypt to a land without water, without food, without shelter, the wilderness experience. And this lasted for forty long years. Because of the wilderness conditions, the Moses generation preferred the past to the promised future in the Promised Land. They desired to return to Egypt and to be subject to slavery just for their daily bread. For them bread was more important to vision and purpose.
I was raised up in a country were personal profit was more valuable to national development and the wellbeing of the community. Many sought after their own wellbeing even to the destruction of the system. We are called for something much more than bread and wine. We have destinies to fulfill and generations to save. We have a course to pursue and a future to seek after. Our mission is all that the Lord has promised us, to possess and to subdue all the Promised Land for the glory of our God.

For the Moses generation, since Egypt seemed to be better than their temporal situation in the wilderness; there was no need to press on for their dreamed future. They all died without seeing the fulfillment of the prophecies and covenants of blessings and prosperity.

The Moses generation was a generation of people that wondered round and round in the same place for forty years without making any tangible progress. You must progress in life in the name of Jesus. It is a curse to spend all your years in the same situation without any improvement and positive change. You have to move forward and not backward. Begin to see yourself advancing towards your promised land. Your future is a land flowing with milk and honey and not the wilderness.

Develop your faith for the blessings and goodness of God to fully manifest in your life and family in every area. Denounce the life of pain, strife and tension. He took you out from the pit of sin and death to take you through unto abundant life.

The Moses generation is that generation of people that were born in suffering and in bondage and they all died in wilderness. It is awful to begin life in pain and poverty and end in a worse condition. The future should be better than the past and present in the name of Jesus. I speak into your situation today: your future will be better than the past and present, as long as you stand still in obedience to the faithful word of God for your life and future. All things can fail but the word of the Lord will surely come to pass in your life.

The Moses generation is that generation that was afraid of their enemy. They called their enemies Giants. They made themselves victims without even an attempt to fight their enemies. Can you begin to see yourself more than conqueror? See your enemy under you and never over you. Have the faith to confront your enemy and you will see them confounded and defeated in the name of Jesus Christ.
Let no diagnosis bring fear in your heart, your God is well able and greater than any challenge in your life.

Don't be shaken by what you hear in the news: you are standing on the Rock that cannot be shaken. Jesus is the eternal Rock of ages; build your life on him and stand to face the storms of life with courage and assurance.
My wife was diagnosed with arthritis; she suffered terribly, and looked twice older than her real age. She experienced severe pain in her joints. As we consulted the doctor, the report was

frightening and we had no money for the expensive drugs. As days went by her pains increased and it came to the point that she could not even lift up a bucket of water. One night we decided to put the word of God in practice, we held our hands and denounced arthritis in the name of Jesus. She began to confess healing scriptures and built her faith in the promises of the Bible. You know what? We did not even know the day she was healed, she forgot that she was sick and until this day she has no traces of Arthritis. She is completely healed in the name of Jesus.

Refuse to be shaken by your financial or job situation, put your trust in the name of Jesus Christ the Son of God. Exercise your faith in the promises of the Bible. God will surely do what He said he would do.

The Moses generation is that generation of people that confessed doubts and fear instead of faith and trust in God. Because of fear and unbelief they died with unfulfilled dreams and unrealized projects. They died on the way; they came close to, but could not enter in. They magnified their enemies instead of magnifying the God of their salvation.

See how big your God is. He is a great, great God, nothing to be compared to Him. See your God well able to do it for you. Never see your troubles as though they are impossible situations, God can, just believe it. Never provoke God through unbelief, have faith in the Lord Jesus Christ for the miraculous. Have faith in His word, your works without faith can never save you.

"Lord Jesus I set myself free from weakness mentality and from victim mentality. I am a covenant child and there is a divine promise upon my life that must be fulfilled in due time. Lord help me to accept the provision you have made for my complete victory over every enemy of my life and destiny. Today I make up my mind that I will not die in the wilderness; I must enter my promised land. I will be a partaker of every blessing in the Promised Land, I press on for my inheritance, in the name of the Lord Jesus Christ," Amen.

The Joshua Generation

Joshua is the man that led the children of Israel from the wilderness to the Promised Land. He led a generation of people that were all born in the wilderness but were determined not to remain or die in the wilderness. They were all consumed with the zeal to press on and to fight to possess all the land that is promised to their fathers. They were willing to go beyond the limitations and weaknesses of the past generations. This is a generation that refuses to be influenced negatively by the example of their fathers. They refused to be negatively influenced by the philosophies of the past generation.

We know the truth and the truth has set us free.
Know the truth that greater is He that is in us than he that is in the world.
We know the truth that our future is better than the past.
We know the truth that no weapon formed against us shall prosper.
We know the truth that a thousand shall fall on our left and ten thousands on our right hand. Pestilence shall not come near our dwelling place.

We know the truth that we are unstoppable by the forces of the evil one. We have the authority to trample on serpents and on scorpions in the name of Jesus Christ.

We know the truth that darkness and weeping is but for a season, joy comes in the morning. God will turn things around for our testimony.

The Joshua generation is a generation that learned discipline in the wilderness. The wilderness was a training ground for the Joshua generation. They prepared themselves physically, spiritually and mentally for the battles of the Promised Land. Your difficult days are meant to prepare you for your better days ahead. Until you experience financial difficulties you will never appreciate, and handle your investments and achievement cautiously. When you fall don't just struggle to stand up, learn how to remain standing by knowing what caused you to fall. Never remain where you fell, stand up and keep going.

The Joshua generation is that generation that had a forward vision and not backward vision. They looked forward and upward and not backward and downward. I and my family made up our minds to look forward to the things that are ahead of us, that which we have to accomplish in life and the goals and visions we must seek to realize instead of dwelling on past mistakes and failures. Whenever you look behind you will see discouragement, which is not the will of God for you. When you look forward you will see purpose and a future to reach out for. Today, reach out by faith to the reason for your living. Jesus will help you get to your expected goal in life.

The Joshua generation was grateful for the daily manna from heaven but were ever anxious for the Promised Land. Nothing could replace or kill their vision for the Promised Land. They did not allow distractions to keep them away from their one goal in life. You need not be distracted, stay focused, remain committed to your course and be determined to go through until you celebrate the victory.

The Joshua generation was not a murmuring and complaining generation. They refused to put the blame on Moses or Aaron, but they decided to motivate themselves and to dedicate themselves anew unto God for mercy and grace in order to make their dream come true.
The Joshua generation was a believing generation. They had the faith that they will face their enemies in battle and conquer them, in order to possess their inheritance. And by faith they crossed over their last obstacle, the Jordan River. The same wilderness that killed the Moses generation could not kill them; instead it prepared them and strengthened them for warfare. I speak into your life today; your season to cross over every obstacle in your life has come in the name of Jesus Christ. The barriers that your parents could not overcome must give way for you in Jesus name. I see you crossing the last obstacle to your breakthrough. I see you crossing the last obstacle to your wedding in the name of Jesus. Begin to see yourself crossing the barriers that the past generation could not cross in every area of your life.

In my family amongst my brothers and sisters, almost every body is a drop out from school; no body has attended school and successfully graduated from high school. I refused to accept what limited my siblings; I pressed on against all odds and last month I got my Masters Degree in Ministry. If no one has ever succeeded in your family, you will be the first to succeed. Believe that you can do it through Christ Jesus that is in you.

The Joshua generation took over the land systematically and progressively through offensive warfare, they attacked their enemies. Those who seek to fight defensive warfare always end up as victims. There are always two ways to deal with your enemies, if you seek to avoid an attack; either you attack or you make peace with the enemy. In the kingdom of God there is no room for negotiation with the devil. There is room for political negotiations, for social peace and security. There is no common ground to negotiate with the enemy of your soul, except you compromise your moral and spiritual values. Rebuke the devil and he will flee. Never negotiate your soul for anything.

The Joshua generation was a generation that believed in women's ministry in the kingdom of God. For the spies were rescued by Rahab of Jericho. Who became a blessed mother in the linage of the Messiah. The kingdom of God can never prosper without the active ministry of women who are sanctified, anointed and called to be a blessing in the body of Christ. Every ministry that restricts women from ministry will end up in traditions, oppression and in religion.
The Joshua generation was that generation of men and women of God with the promise of divine backing and divine authority. "Every place that the sole of your feet shall tread, I give unto you".*

The Joshua generation was a generation that believed in the power of praise and worship. The walls of Jericho tumbled as the praised and worshiped God with shouts of victory. Anointed Praise and worship will always create an atmosphere for the power of God to manifest. Wise kings go to war with praise and worship leaders going ahead of them singing and giving glory to God. Develop praise and worship as a lifestyle; sing unto the Lord at all times, give all the glory and honor to him who is seated on the right hand of God.

Singing heals, it sets one free from stress and fills our hearts with the presence of the Holy Spirit.
King David who wrote most of the psalms, wrote them in times of great difficulties, learn to sing even if you are in a cave surrounded by your enemies. Let nothing stop you from singing unto the Lord.

The Joshua generation was that generation that had the keys of success. "This book of the law shall not depart out of thy mouth; but thou shalt meditate therein day and night, that thou mayest observe to do according to all that is written therein: for then thou shalt make thy way prosperous, and then thou shalt have good success".*

Their secret for success was faith in the word, walking in obedience to the word. Believing and confessing the word, being in conformity with the word of God.
Faith in the word of God will bring life, honor, prosperity and peace in your life and family. It will take faith to act upon what God has said. It will take faith to stand upon God's promises in times of trials and great challenges. It is faith in the word that disarms our enemies, trust in yourself effort and man made solutions will fail you and only worsen your situation.

The Joshua generation was that generation that experienced the fulfillment of the promises of God. They believed and the possessed the land. They possessed their God given inheritance through warfare. You will possess it, you will subdue and you will inherit that which you have believed and had faith for. The children of Israel finally possessed the land flowing with milk and honey, they had houses they did not build and farms they did not plant, because God rewarded all their years in the wilderness.

I speak unto you in the name of the Lord; that your years of pain and hardship will be rewarded a hundred fold as long as you remain faithful to the word of God. In Christ our future is assured, our days are blessed because of the blood of the new covenant. The blood of Jesus Christ the righteous has broken every barrier and has made a new and living way for us; we are the blessed of the Lord.
Tell yourself and confess it aloud; I am the blessed of the Lord, my days are blessed.

What the Lord did in times past and for others, He is able to do it today and for you.
Have the faith that he can do it even now:
Your healing is possible today and even now.
Your complete deliverance, personal or family deliverance is possible.
Your salvation from every sin and the force of addiction is possible today and now.
Your protection and total security is possible in Christ.
Miracles still happen and God can do it even now.
Your restoration and revival is available at your will, even now.

Jesus is willing to intervene for your job, your marriage, your children, your home and your finances even right now.
It can happen today and now to those who believe and put their trust in him. Joshua believed God and it worked for him; it will

work for you and for me as we put our faith in the Lord God of our salvation.

I come to announce to you today that God's covenant promises will work out for good in your life; only believe.

MEDITATION

What Love will not do.

- Love does not neglect - Love cares, love is care. Love is concern.
- Love does not condemn and discourage – Love supports, love is ever present to help.
- Love does not pretend – Love is real, Love is transparent, Love is sincere, Love is simple and not complicated.
- Love cannot be hidden – Love manifest, Love reveals, love demonstrates.
- Love cannot think evil – Love seeks the wellbeing of others, Love offers utmost delight and comfort. Love is pure.
- Love cannot hold back, or keep back – Love shares, love gives out.
- Love cannot listen to gossips and backbiting – Love defends, love protects, love believes all things. Love trust.
- Love does not offend – Love consoles, Love heals, love feels the pain of others.
- Love does not oppress, Love does not despise, Love does not limit people – Love promotes, Love liberates, Love motivates.
- Love does not separate – Love unites, love reconciles, Love builds intimacy.
- Love does not end in sweet words – Love acts, Love performs.
- Love cannot cause you to refuse food. Love fellowships together, Lovers eat together.
- Love cannot keep you out of home for too long – love dwells at home. Love spends quality time at home.

- Love does not spend its money foolishly – Love invests in children education and the wellbeing of the family. Love is not stupid.
- Love does not have seasons – Love is always, Love is constant.
- Love does not stay in silence – love communicates.
- Love does not nurse bitterness and pain – Love forgives.
- Love does not give room for external influence to determine its actions – Love is certain, Love is assured, Love is unstoppable.
- Love never runs out of time – Love always makes time available, Love will never say, "I don't have time for you".
- Love does not offer stress and headaches – Love offers solutions and pleasure. Love shares with your stress and headaches.
- Love does not seek its own profit – Love seeks the best for the other.
- You can heal hearts, give hope, and wipe tears and save souls through love.
- Let the Love of Jesus Christ cause you to walk and manifest true love for one another.
- Grow in love. Let our families and communities be a lovely environment for our children to grow in love.

CHAPTER EIGHT

Walking In Divine Authority

"Behold, I give unto you power to tread on serpents and scorpions, and over all the power of the enemy: and nothing shall by any means hurt you.

Not withstanding in this rejoice not, that the spirits are subject unto you; but rather rejoice, because your names are written in heaven".*

THE MEANING OF AUTHORITY

Authority is the faith to stand in the face of challenges. David stood the ground and faced Goliath the philistine giant. While others were confused and full of fear, young anointed David surprisingly stepped forward for the challenge.

A man with divine authority will refuse to run, running can never change anything, trying to run away from difficulties and responsibilities only serve to plunge us deeper into more hardship. With the authority of the word and the Holy Spirit in us we have what it takes to face the winds and the temptations of life. We have what it takes to stand our testing moments and to cause our mountains to become beautiful plains. We are called to stand until we produce triumphs and testimonies in the midst of tribulations.

A man with divine authority will refuse to hide. Who are you seeking to hide from and why? When others are hiding because of fear, we boldly stand to face the situation and to push back the enemy with the sword of the Spirit and the word of our testimony. Come out from your hiding place, it is time to face the facts and to make a difference in our community. We refuse to be cowards and to draw back; we are fit for the task. As long as the oceans can never be afraid of the waves, so we should never be afraid of the battles of life. People who seek for avenues to hide will subsequently seek for means to escape from challenging situations. That which you seek to avoid due to fear, will render you void of power and authority.

Make a decision to stand to face it in your home and marriage, stand and face it in your business ventures. Face the challenges of your career, you have what it takes to overcome and to celebrate breakthroughs in the name of Jesus Christ.
Face life with boldness and assurance.
Decide to face life with a winning mentality.

Authority is the certification of your position in Christ.

You need to be a certified child of God, washed by the blood of Jesus Christ and sanctified by the word of God. As a child of God I have divine authority. My heavenly father has placed His hand on me saying fear not, I am with you always.
I am a certified servant of God. As a servant of God I am backed by divine authority. The Spirit of the Lord is upon me.

Tell yourself; the Lord is with me, "if God is with me, who can be against me".
I'm a certified Son of God. As a son a God I am empowered by divine privileges. You touch me you touch trouble. As a son of God, I carry covenant blessings.

As a son of God, angels work for my good and safety. Angels are assigned for my wellbeing. I'm a certified believer and as a believer in Jesus Christ; all things are possible through faith in His name. Mountains become plains, valleys are filled, and the crooked paths become straight. The impossible become possible. It shall be possible for you as you discover your authority as a child of God. It is possible; is the language of men and women of faith. In Christ Jesus no situation is hopeless and final; God can turn things around for a testimony. Change is possible, deliverance is possible.

It is possible to be filled with the Holy Spirit. It is possible to live sanctified and holy in the midst of a perverse and wicked generation. It is possible to make a difference with our lifestyle and our new man in Christ. Wipe out "impossibility" from your vocabulary. Our God can and wants to do it for you; do you believe in a new beginning through Christ? He is able to make all things new according to His word.

Your visa for your next level in life is possible. Begin to celebrate your desired future by conceiving and meditating on its reality and possibility.
Your wedding is possible and a fruitful marital life is possible.

Your dreamed job is possible and your financial miracle is possible. Do you believe it can all happen to you just as the scripture said it?
Your healing and healthy living is possible. God wants you to enjoy good health and soundness. Sickness and afflictions are never His will for you; prepare your mind to live in soundness mentally and socially. Refuse a sick head and a sick heart.
Your promotion is possible; See yourself advancing in life economically and spiritually. Seek the Lord for wisdom for tangible achievements and breakthrough. Believe God for uncommon testimonies.

Your restoration is possible; your God can still do what He did for Job, bringing back a hundred fold blessing. All that you ever lost can be restored, it is possible. The life of joy and peace is still possible, welcome by faith the joy of the Lord into your heart.

Shout… It is possible, I am a believer, I believe it.

In Christ we are certified by the blood of Jesus. His blood on the cross qualified us for every blessing and grace in this life and eternity. We are certified by the baptism of the Holy Spirit: "And these signs shall follow them that believe; in my name shall they cast out devils; they shall speak with new tongues: They shall take up serpents; and if they drink any deadly thing, it shall not hurt them; they shall lay hands on the sick, and they shall recover".*

The Holy Spirit Baptism is the key to the believer's victory and an uncommon lifestyle. Abide in him and grow in the Holy Spirit. Develop intimacy with the Holy Spirit for your fullness of life and peace.

A child of God is certified by the word of God. We live by the word of God and believe every word of God. The word of God is the life of the believer. Without the word everything dies. Our faith feeds on the word of God. As long as you remain faithful to the word; the promise of God for your life will come to pass.

Authority is the acknowledgement of your qualification and your personality.

Confess these sentences aloud.
I am a qualified child of God by the grace of God.
I am qualified by the blood of Jesus Christ that was shed on the cross for my sins.
I am qualified for the blessings of God through my faith in the blood of the New Covenant; Jesus became a curse that I might inherit the blessings of Abraham through faith.

I am qualified for healing through the stripes of Jesus.

I am qualified for prosperity, for he has made me an heir of God. All that belongs to God belongs to me.
I am qualified for eternal life through the gift of salvation by faith in Jesus Christ the Son of God.
I am qualified for peace of mind in a troubled world, for He said; "My peace I give to you, not as the world giveth".*
I am qualified for abundant life; for He Jesus my Lord is the source of abundant life, He came to give life in abundance.
I am qualified for victorious living through the blood of Jesus Christ.
I am qualified for a better life here on earth and for eternal life in the name of Jesus Christ.
I am qualified for heaven because my name is written in the book of life by grace.
Begin to thank God for your quality and eternal life in Christ.

Be thankful for your secured life in Christ.
Give glory to God for your free divine protection.
In Christ we can boldly say; we are free from the power of darkness in the name of Jesus.
In Christ we walk in authority; through Christ we reign in life.
It is not by power or by might, not by academic qualifications; not by financial achievements but by the blood of Jesus Christ the Son of God.

Are you qualified?
Religion can never qualify us, nor can good works.
Church membership can never qualify us.
Only the blood of Jesus, the sinless blood of the only Son of God; has the power to wash us and to cleanse us before God.
We are qualified through the precious blood of Jesus Christ.

Authority is submission to God.
No true submission no through authority.
I submit to the will of God.
I submit to the leading of the Holy Spirit of God.
I submit to godly authority.
I submit to the word of God.
Just make up your mind to submit from your heart and you will see the difference it will make in your life.
As a young man growing up with no father and a poor mother who could not take care nor provide for my needs; I became stubborn and disobedient. I wanted to control myself and did not want to follow any instruction from any body. I soon realized that the more I was stubborn the more things became hard on me and the more I failed. I realized once I accepted correction and was humble to learn and to be submissive the more I succeeded and performed well in every area. And through the grace of God I became born-again and surrendered to Christ Jesus. I learned that submission and obedience was profitable in every area of life.
I now submit to the word of God from my heart.

When you submit He will raise you up.
When you submit He will make a way for you.
When you submit He will empower you for life.
When you submit He will fill you with his presence and power.
Abraham submitted to God and he became a blessing to the whole world.
Moses submitted to God, he became the deliverer of Israel.

Joshua submitted, he became the one to lead Israel to the promised land.
David submitted he became the king of Israel.

Esther submitted she became the queen of Persia.
Elisha submitted to Elijah and he received the double portion of the Anointing.
Your submission will cause you to receive from God.
Today is your day to submit to God and to receive.
You will receive healing from every disease.
You will receive deliverance from every power of the enemy.
You will receive wisdom for uncommon success.
You will receive power over all your fears in Jesus name.

Authority is divine backing.
Remember Elijah and the prophets of Baal; the prophets of Baal had no backing from their god and they could not have any result no matter how long they prayed and cried. Elijah was different; he did not struggle to get divine results because the Lord God of Israel was with him.
Abraham was backed by God and his life and testimony full of divine encounters with God. He was victorious and successful in every thing he did.

Moses was backed by God, for no human being will ever dare to stand before king Pharaoh, to challenge him and get out alive. All the signs and wonders performed by Moses in Egypt confirmed that the God of Israel was with him.
Joseph was backed by God, for he was favored by God in every stage of his life. And because of his faith and trust in His God, God raised him up in a strange land to the second in command.

Daniel was backed by God and the Lions could not eat him. The plans of all his enemies failed.

The three Hebrew boys were backed by God, fire could not consume them and as a result; the king turned to the God of Israel because he saw and believed that God was with them.
Peter was backed by God, his shadow healed the sick and the angel opened the prison doors for his deliverance.

When God back's you up; no demon can oppress you and no darkness can overcome you.
No witch can hinder you and no human wickedness can succeed against you.
When God back's you, you will stand and face the forces of the enemy with boldness and confidence.
Today your pursuers will be pursued because the Lord is with you.
Every power that pursued you, must bow before the presence of the Lord your God.
David was backed by God, he had authority and the boldness to face and to kill and to cut off the head of Goliath. He could not do it without the tangible presence of the Lord with him.

You will kill the Goliath pursuing your family.
Today, your long-term enemy must bow.
The forces of the wicked that had power over you must be conquered and be under your feet in the name of Jesus Christ.
Today every yoke must be broken.

Today, power has changed hands in the name of Jesus.
Your spiritual oppressors must be oppressed and become victims.
The enemy must be conquered and the strongholds must be broken.

Take authority today in the name of Jesus Christ.
Deliver your self through the blood of Jesus.

Declare the deliverance of your family from every negative influence. Declare the deliverance of your business from every spiritual attacks intended to slow down your business breakthrough.

Speak forth the deliverance of your office and place of work from every form of witchcraft and occult's practices. Seal your office with the blood of Jesus. No wicked plans to take your place and to hinder your success will succeed in the name of Jesus Christ.

Speak deliverance of your finances and wealth. Call forth your wealth to come forth, declare that your labor will not be in vain. The works of your hands will bring forth great financial benefits. Rebuke every financial devourer and close every unwanted way the enemy wants to drain your finances.

Deliver your destiny from satanic influence. Declare over and over that your days are blessed and your future is better than your past and present.

Deliver your compound and neighborhood from crimes and insecurity. Deliver your town and city from disasters and misfortunes. Stand in the gap as an intercessor for the peace of your community. Deliver your inheritance from the hands of the wicked. You will not labor for the wicked to inherit, and by faith reach out to your God-given inheritance in Christ.

Declare your prosperity and reject poverty and hardship. Declare your life free from bondage. When the Son of God set you free, you are free indeed.

Take your authority and declare total deliverance.
Today take charge; Reign over the enemy.
Break every satanic family alters. Break every bloodline curse. Break every soul ties that are working against your life.

Break every force of jealousy that is speaking against your success and promotion in life.

Break and destroy every force of the wicked one that has been standing on your way in past years. Declare your season for total breakthrough and manifestation has come; the set time for the manifestation of the sons of God has come. Let no darkness overshadow you anymore. The time for your testimony to fully manifest has come in the name of Jesus Christ.

There is power, mighty power in the blood of Jesus Christ.

Authority is victorious living.
You were born to walk and to live victorious.
You were born to win your life's battles and to celebrate victory.
You must regain supernatural victory. Your victory is a must.
You must win in life. Tell yourself: I must win in life in the name Jesus.

We need to exercise our authority in all areas of life.

Take authority over the forces of sin and death.
Take authority over the power of sickness and disease.
Take authority over occultism and Satanism in your community.
Subdue the power of evil in your community.
Take authority over every form of addictions.
Take authority over all forms and causes of fears.
Overcome your limitations by your faith in the supernatural ability of the Holy Spirit working within you.

Walk in authority by the power of the word of God within you.

"Ye *are* blessed of the LORD which made heaven and earth. The heaven, *even* the heavens, *are* the LORD'S: but the earth hath he given to the children of men".*

"Thou shalt not be afraid for the terror by night; *nor* for the arrow *that* flieth by day; *Nor* for the pestilence *that* walketh in darkness; *nor* for the destruction *that* wasteth at noonday.

A thousand shall fall at thy side, and ten thousand at thy right hand; *but* it shall not come nigh thee. Only with thine eyes shalt thou behold and see the reward of the wicked.

Because thou hast made the LORD, *which is* my refuge, *even* the most High, thy habitation.

There shall no evil befall thee, neither shall any plague come nigh thy dwelling. For he shall give his angels charge over thee, to keep thee in all thy ways.

They shall bear thee up in *their* hands, lest thou dash thy foot against a stone. Thou shalt tread upon the lion and adder: the young lion and the dragon shalt thou trample under feet.

Because he hath set his love upon me, therefore will I Deliver him: I will set him on high, because he hath known my name. He shall call upon me, and I will answer him: I *will be* with him in trouble; I will deliver him, and honour him. With long life will I satisfy him, and shew him my salvation".*

CHAPTER NINE

Prospering in crisis times

This is the right time for your uncommon success.
Tell yourself with confidence, 'my season has come'.

Isaac prospered in times of famine.

"Then Isaac sowed in that land, and received in the same year an hundredfold: and the LORD blessed him.
And the man waxed great, and went forward, and grew until he became very great:
For he had possession of flocks, and possession of herds, and great store of servants: and the Philistines envied him".*

Isaac sowed his seeds trusting God for the results and he got it. The Lord blessed his hard work and rewarded him with a hundred fold harvest. Sow in season and out of season. The harvest you need is in the seeds you have, timely sow your seeds with absolute faith and trust in God. He will do it for you.

Joseph prospered when no one could solve the king's dilemma.
King Pharaoh's problems took Joseph from prison to the palace.

"Then Pharaoh sent and called Joseph, and they brought him hastily out of the dungeon: and he shaved *himself,* and changed his raiment, and came in unto Pharaoh.
And Pharaoh said unto Joseph, I have dreamed a dream, and there *is* none that can interpret it: and I have heard say of thee, *that* thou canst understand a dream to interpret it.
And Joseph answered Pharaoh, saying, *It is* not in me: God shall give Pharaoh an answer of peace".*

The problems you solve will be the key to your prosperity. God will cause you to bring an answer to someone's problem that will open to you a new door and give you a platform for a new beginning. Like Joseph his story changed overnight, God can do it for you. Every problem you solve takes you forward in life and makes you distinguished. The trouble of Pharaoh was a lifetime opportunity for Joseph, and he maximized the moment, he acted wisely and transformed his lifetime. He became the first and only Jewish prime minister in Egypt.

The children of Israel prospered in the midst of the greatest crisis in Egypt.
When the families of Egypt had lost their first born, then God asked them to go and ask for gold, and every precious thing.

"And Pharaoh rose up in the night, he and all his servants and all the Egyptians; and there was a great cry in Egypt; for *there was* not a house where *there was* not one dead. And he called for Moses and Aaron by night, and said, rise up, *and* get you forth from among my people, both ye and the children of Israel;

and go, serve the LORD, as ye have said. Also take your flocks and your herds, as ye have said, and begone; and bless me also. And the Egyptians were urgent upon the people, that they might send them out of the land in haste; for they said, we *be* all dead *men*. And the people took their dough before it was leavened, their kneading troughs being bound up in their clothes upon their shoulders. And the children of Israel did according to the word of Moses; and they borrowed of the Egyptians jewels of silver, and jewels of gold, and raiment:

And the LORD gave the people favor in the sight of the Egyptians, so that they lent unto them such things as they required. And they spoiled the Egyptians".*

This day marked the end of four hundred and thirty years of the captivity of the Israelites. But they did not leave empty handed, they left rich in gold and silver. The years of their vain and painful labor were rewarded in one day. They prospered in the midst of the weeping and crying of the people of Egypt.

Today; I hear the cry of the world, every where the news is the same: poverty, crisis, bankruptcy, disasters, terrorism and fears. But we are the chosen of the God, those who walk by faith and not by sight. We smile and rejoice for our source of wealth is not based on the world's economic system. We are children of the Most high God and all the silver and the gold belong to our God and we are heirs of God through Christ Jesus our Lord.

The world is too rich for God's children to be poor. Connect to the Lord and you will see the difference. The word of the Lord is the greatest wealth in the whole universe; fill your life with 'thus said the Lord'. His world will produce in you the character you need to manage wealth with a healthy and sound mind.

David got a lifetime breakthrough on battle ground.
He killed Goliath the nation's oppressor and terrorist and his story changed for life.

"And it came to pass, when the Philistine arose, and came and drew nigh to meet David, that David hasted, and ran toward the army to meet the Philistine.
And David put his hand in his bag, and took thence a stone, and slang *it,* and smote the Philistine in his forehead that the stone sunk into his forehead; and he fell upon his face to the earth. So David prevailed over the Philistine with a sling and with a stone, and smote the Philistine, and slew him; but *there was* no sword in the hand of David".*

Goliath; that great challenge you seem to face at the moment. That mountain that seem insurmountable, that report that seems to be irreversible. That situation that sounds humanly impossible.
The time for your Goliath to bow has come, begin to celebrate the defeat of every form of Goliath that has resisted and obstructed your dream for several years.

Esther prospered in crisis time in Persia.
Though Esther was an orphan, a stranger in the land and in captivity, she made use of the opportunity created by Vashti.

"So Esther was taken unto king Ahasuerus into his house royal in the tenth month, which *is* the month Tebeth, in the seventh year of his reign. And the king loved Esther above all the women, and she obtained grace and favour in his sight more than all the virgins; so that he set the royal crown upon her head, and made her queen instead of Vashti.

Then the king made a great feast unto all his princes and his servants, *even* Esther's feast; and he made a release to the provinces, and gave gifts, according to the state of the king".*

Make use of the open doors that are available before you today; don't disqualify yourself, trust God.
Esther believed God and against all odds was enlisted by faith. God will be glorified through the steps of faith you take towards realizing your dream. Cast away all fears and human discouragements press on by faith in the name of Jesus.
Remember that you are favored by the Lord and his glory that is upon you will make you unique. No one can close the doors that your God opens for you, but you have to walk into them by faith.

Daniel and his three friends prospered and where promoted when the king issued a death sentence to all the wise men of Babylon.
The king and the whole kingdom were greatly shaken, until Daniel came before the king with the answer. The result was uncommon promotion.

"The king answered unto Daniel, and said, of a truth *it is,* that your God *is* a God of gods, and a Lord of kings, and a revealer of secrets, seeing thou couldest reveal this secret.

Then the king made Daniel a great man, and gave him many great gifts, and made him ruler over the whole province of Babylon, and chief of the governors over all the wise *men* of Babylon. Then Daniel requested of the king, and he set

Shadrach, Meshach, and Abednego, over the affairs of the province of Babylon: but Daniel *sat* in the gate of the king'.*

Can you imagine how the children of Israel felt with the promotion of their own sons to prominent positions in a foreign land? In difficult times God would always provide a way out by raising an anointed person with the keys for change and victory. You have what it takes for change and victory; you have what it takes for breakthrough and development. Make use of what is in your hand and what ever you do, give it your best.

In this season, you are a chosen figure and an appointed individual with answers to the questions of this generation. Don't despise yourself; see your life changing positively even in difficult times. Begin to affect change in your family and community; you were not born to be a burden but a blessing.

Peter's breakthrough and prosperity came in the moment of his greatest failure, the night he caught nothing was the same day he got more than enough.
Peter was washing his net to go home with an empty boat, when suddenly Jesus requested to use his boat. And at the end of the ministry session, Peter was leaving with two boats of fish.*

When you think that all is lost, that might be the turning point. Peter experienced an uncommon turn around in his business career, almost when he was about signing out; he got the surprising lifetime breakthrough. It's never too late for God's favor to take you forward. This is the time for God to turn things around you for good. In your home things will turn around for good. In your financial situation, it will turn around for good. In your place of work, God will make it a blessing. In your marriage, God will make it a place to be.

Your relationship will be healed and restored completely. Your love life will blossom all over again. In your career, see breakthrough and in your moral and spiritual life things are turning round for your testimony.

Never lose focus on your dream, no matter the seasons and times. For Peter it happened at the close of the day.

When the multitude had nothing but a lad's provision of five loaves and two fish; Jesus turned their story around and the leftover was twelve baskets full after feeding more than five thousand people.*

From nothing to abundance is the story of the redeemed of the Lord. Make it your testimony; accept the finished work of Jesus Christ on the cross for your inheritance and divine covenant possession.

In Christ, you have been diagnosed success positive and there is nothing the devil can do about it.

NOTES

Chapter one
1. Isaiah. 61:3
2. Deuteronomy. 7:6.
3. Jeremiah. 31:3
4. Galatians. 5:9
5. Ephesians. 1:18-19.
6. Hebrews. 7:25.
7. Ephesians. 6:12
8. Isaiah. 54:17.
9. Luke. 10:18-19
10. Romance. 8:14.
11. 2 Corinthians. 3:6.
12. Isaiah. 61:1.
13. John. 14:17.
14. John. 14:23-24.
15. John. 5:32.
16. Luke. 1:35
17. Luke. 9:34
18. Exodus. 24:18.
19. Psalm. 30.
20. Psalm. 115:12-16

Chapter Two
1. Genesis. 1:26-28.

2. Joshua 2: 8-15.
3. Matthew. 1:5.
4. Joshua 9: 3-15.
5. Genesis. 30:31-39.
6. 1 Kings. 3: 24-28.
7. 2 Samuel. 17:7-14.
8. Esther. 7:1-10.
9. Esther. 7: 10
10. 2 Samuel. 12: 1-6.
11. Jeremiah. 29:11. (Paraphrased).
12. Genesis. 21:19
13. Genesis. 30:37-39.
14. Genesis. 22:13

Chapter Three
1. Isaiah. 9:6-7.
2. Colossians. 2/9-10.
3. John. 1:14
4. John. 3:34-35.
5. 2 Corinthians. 4:4
6. Colossians. 1:15
7. Hebrews. 1:3
8. 1 Corinthians. 1:23-24
9. John. 8:12
10. John. 9:5
11. John. 11:25
12. Genesis. 3:15.
13. Isaiah 7:14.
14. Isaiah 53:7-9.

Chapter Four
1. 1 Chronicles 4:9-10.

Chapter Five.
1. Genesis. 4:13-15
2. Genesis. 4:15.
3. Romance. 3:23, 6:23.
4. Exodus. 2:15
5. Hebrews. 11:31
6. James. 2:25.
7. Matthew. 1:5.
8. Luke. 5:1-10
9. Psalm. 1:1-6.
10. Acts 7: 55-56.
11. Isaiah. 6:1.
12. Deuteronomy. 28:12.
13. Romance. 10:13.
14. Proverbs. 11:25

Chapter Six.
1. Ezekiel 19:1-9
2. Judges16: 20-21.
3. Genesis. 40:3.
4. Genesis. 37:3.
5. Daniel. 6: 16-24.
6. Psalm. 124:7

Chapter seven
1. Joshua. 1:1-8
2. Joshua. 1:3.
3. Joshua. 1:8.

Chapter Eight.
1. Luke. 10:19-20
2. Make 16:17-18

3. John. 14: 27.
4. Psalm. 115: 15-16.
5. Psalm. 91:4-16.

Chapter Nine
1. Genesis. 26:12-14. {Read the complete story Gen 26:1-14}.
2. Genesis. 41/14-16
3. Genesis.12:30-36.
4. 1 Samuel. 17:48-50
5. Esther 2/16-18.
6. Daniel 2: 47-49.
7. Read Luke. 5:1-11.
8. Matthew. 14:17-20.

The Author will be pleased to hear from you and to share with your joy and testimony after reading this book.

Contact:
Dr Bonnie Etta.
Email: agborbonnie@gmail.com
Facebook: Dr Bonnie Etta

ABOUT THE AUTHOR

Dr Bonnie Etta is the senior pastor and founder of the World Mission international Worship Center in Maryland- USA and founder of the World Mission Int, Bible College.

He has served in the past forty years in various mission fields in Africa and Europe and his ministry has restored thousands of souls around the world to faith and the power of the Holy Spirit.

Dr Bonnie Etta has authored several inspirational books including the best selling: "**STREE FREE LIFE, Lord Use Me**" Etc. Check for Books by Dr Bonnie Etta of Amazon.

ABOUT THE BOOK

"Becoming your dream" is inspirational, prophetic and full of life and wisdom. It will certainly take you to a new level in life.

Your long term dream can become reality. "When you think that all is lost, that might be your turning point". Your future can be recreated, restored and regained. See it, believe it, take steps toward it and trust God for it. This is a book to read and be ready for a miracle.

Bonnie Etta, PhD

www.ingramcontent.com/pod-product-compliance
Lightning Source LLC
Chambersburg PA
CBHW061736070526
44585CB00024B/2701